GATHERING IN THE NAMES

GATHERING IN THE NAMES

MICHAEL ORTIZ HILL
and
AUGUSTINE KANDEMWA

A Journey into the Land of African Gods

WITH AN AFTERWORD
BY
DEENA METZGER

SPRING JOURNAL BOOKS
WOODSTOCK, CONNECTICUT

Africa Series 2

Gathering in the Names
© 2002 Michael Ortiz Hill and the Nganga Project
All rights reserved

"Afterword"
© 2002 Deena Metzger
All rights reserved

First Edition printing 2002;
Spring Journal Books

Published by Spring Audio & Journal, Inc.;
299 East Quassett Road;
Woodstock, Connecticut 06281

Printed by BookMasters;
Mansfield, Ohio

Text printed on acidfree paper

Cover and book designed by JFL

Library in Congress Cataloging in Publication Data
Pending

Whenever two or more of you
are gathered in my name,
there I am among you.

Matthew 18: 20

The world I love is in great
need of healing, and I am incapable
of healing it. Please help me.

The Beggars Prayer
by Deena Metzger

Contents

I

SERVING THE SPIRITS
INTRODUCTION

Several years ago my study of dreams brought me to write about the situation of racism in America. I was compelled by the idea that African-American dreams could be understood from the wisdom tradition at their source, and so I began exploring the African origins of black American culture. Eventually I went to Africa and met the Bantu healer, Augustine Kandemwa, in Zimbabwe.

To our surprise, as Augustine initiated me into the medicine tradition of his people, a mystery began to open up between us. I call this mystery "gathering in the names" to offer a twist of sweet plurality to Jesus's insight: Whenever two or more are gathered in the name of the sacred, spirit descends, awakens, transforms. This book is the story of two men who have taken up this work of "gathering" even while the world disintegrates in its relentless way. It is also a story of surrender or, as they say in Africa, "initiation." And finally it is a story of two men from different worlds who have come to call each other "twin brother."

There were two moments in my first initiation with Augustine that especially invited us into this mystery.

After my friend Dr. Richard Kimball introduced me to Augustine as a healer from America, Augustine asked if I read dreams. I admitted that was a large part of what I do and that I also read the Tarot. Without missing a beat he took me into the house of his spirits and had me do a reading. Coming to the obstacle card he had chosen, I tried to explain the Knight of Wands—his bluster and his visionary fire. In the deck I use, this is Bellerophon, the warrior astride his flying horse, Pegasus. Bellerophon believed himself to be invincible until a horsefly bit Pegasus, Pegasus bolted, and Bellerophon was thrown down to the earth. I felt exhausted looking at the card. As one trains over the years to be a healer, one's development depends on confronting interior obstacles. Such was the harsh passage that had prepared me for initiation. I knew Bellerophon all too well.

"Oh, yes," Augustine said. "I know that spirit. Can you chase it out of me? I can cast spirits out of other people, but I can't cast them out of myself." How puzzling it was for me, after four years of being prepared to be initiated, that this African healer would ask that I heal him. After a night of self-scrutiny, I agreed to attempt to meet Augustine's request, and in the morning we entered into what was to become an initiation of one another. Mutual initiation is not exactly a traditional African way, and yet, at the same time, it is consistent with what Augustine calls "initiating by dialogue."

The second moment happened near the end of my initiation when I was fully taken into African culture. The Knight of Wands in me had always lived by the habit of greed, the seemingly inexhaustible hunger to conquer new worlds where, I believed, I could strut my magnificence. Gratitude seems to undo all that, and by the time Augustine and I had arrived on the banks of the Zambezi river to complete the initiation, I had been so welcomed into the African spirit world that to ask for anything more seemed, well, rude.

The core of Shona ethics lies in "serving the spirits" of other people: hospitality to the person before you but quite beyond that, hospitality to the person's ancestral spirits upon whom the welfare of the individual and the community rests. I had in mind only a simple ritual on Augustine's behalf, quietly aligning his spirit with the spirit of the river; but before I began, I climbed into the water to pray. I wanted there to be no taint of egotism. I requested that whatever stood between me and serving Augustine's spirits be washed away.

Augustine's spirits descended. He was trance possessed for the first time. I was quite out of my depth. I had not anticipated that I would initiate this fine soul into a deeper relationship with his ancestors nor could I have imagined that somehow, simultaneously, he could initiate me. His spirits, one after another, took over his body and did the necessary rituals on me to complete my first initiation. I was frightened and so sang songs to the intelligence of the river to carry us where she would. After several hours Augustine reemerged and wept. "I did not know my spirits were so powerful," he said. And I also wept at the beauty of the river and the bitter recognition of the years I had wasted letting arrogance of the knight blind me to the aliveness of the earth.

Since that day, we have been recognized as *mapatya*—twin brothers. Although Augustine and I are twinned, it would be silly to impose an artificial symmetry between his story and mine or, more accurately, between his way of telling his story and my very Western memoir. Symmetry is immediately broken by the fact that autobiography is not a traditional African form. It took some effort to get my dear *mapatya* to sit still and talk into my mini-cassette recorder. The fact that Augustine's story is composed on the tongue and mine is sifted through the various layers of self-consciousness within which the written word thrives, illustrates something of the cultural distance across which Augustine and I recognized our essential twinship.

The Bantu shaman or *nganga* is the "master of the word," and Augustine is eloquent and charismatic in both Shona and English. The translucent direct statement is highly valued among Bantu people. One's cards are laid out on the table, nothing hidden. From that directness, that translucency, a *nganga* like Augustine evaluates his life in relationship to "the others"—those spirits that called him to the practice of healing. And so his story proceeds not so much asking "What is inside of me?", but "What is the community of the living and the dead that I am inside of, that I serve?" As his apprentice, I have learned much from the agility with which Augustine moves between various ethnic worlds—Shona, Ndebele, Bushmen, Tonga, European, Chinese, Hindu, and the worlds of the living and the dead.

My story is written from a different angle, the heart of the narrative asking, "What is inside of me?" and "How is it that this vagrant soul became an African *nganga?*"

I am an alumnus of psychoanalysis. The very years that Augustine was being initiated by an old Ndebele shaman, I was writhing on the analytic couch beneath the benevolent gaze of Dr. John Seeley. The shamanic rite that is a true analysis is a terrible descent by way of story telling to the true stuff of one's interior life.

Such a rite is not African, and becoming a *nganga* has not made me an African man. One of my pleasures with Augustine has been the rich exchange between two different ways of knowing, two different ways of telling a story.

All this being said, we are twinned, from the infections we both acquired in our navels that almost killed us when we were babies to the displacements of our childhoods, from our Christian educations and our later rejections of Christianity to our political awakenings during times of historical turmoil; from the ferocious ordeals that made us healers to that radiant moment when lives lived apart and parallel came together suddenly on the banks of the Zambezi. It would have been so much easier to write a book about Augustine's life story or my own, but it seems that those twin brothers in the village of the ancestors who brought the two of us together have their own story to tell. Augustine's story and my own interweave chapter by chapter; so perhaps between two stories, one story can be heard, a story that belongs to neither him nor me but comes from the spirits that we serve.

Michael Ortiz Hill

II

THE MYSTERY OF TWINSHIP
INTRODUCTION

Before I met Michael I had no twin, no *mapatya*. What happened is that I had a dream when I was being initiated by an Ndebele *nganga*, Mr. Ndlovu. In it I was looking for my brother in the Matopo Hills. I was near the caves at Siloswane. I met people who were coming out of the caves, and I asked them if they had seen my twin brother who is a white man. I went from one cave to another inside the mountain looking for this brother of mine.

Some people said they saw him inside the mountain. So I went inside to find him, but before I found him, I woke up. Michael also was having dreams in America that told him how to recognize his twin, a black man. And Simakuhle, my wife, too had seen Michael many times in her dreams before he arrived. She was told, "One of the sons of this family is coming home." That is the way these spirits work. This is the way it is with family.

So when we met a few years later, we recognized each other. It was surprising, but we had been prepared by our spirits. The way Michael was born and grew up was identical to how I was born and grew up. He almost died when he was born, and I also almost died when I was born. My umbilical cord was rotten. A spirit medium said I had to be taken to the bush where a temporary shelter was made for me. My mother did this, and I survived. Michael also had a rotten cord when he was a baby.

When I look at Michael's life when he was a street kid without a home, I also did not have a home either. I moved from one place to another, being looked after by strangers. At times I would go without food when I was working for these people. Michael also was hungry. So this *mapatya* issue is real, very real.

After I initiated Michael, he in turn initiated me. There was a give-and-take—"Do me service and I do you service." That is the way of twins who are *ngangas*. As twins and *ngangas* we have to do the work together to heal the people together. He is healing people in the United States; I am healing people in Africa. When he comes here, we heal together. This is how our spirits operate.

When I first had a dream about having a twin who was a white man, it was confusing because I thought this was an obstacle in the way of my spirits. Generally speaking Africans do not know that whites have ancestors and can get trance possessed. So when I saw that Michael had some spirits and that white people also had spirits on them, it was quite a shock to me.

Remember when the missionaries came, they said, "Ancestors are no good. They are evil spirits." But to my surprise I see that lots of white people also have ancestors, and they get trance possessed. And there are also *ngangas* who are white people. Now no one can tell me that whites don't have ancestors because I am initiating them, and I am seeing their spirits. It seems possible to me that there are no human beings without ancestor spirits upon them.

As soon as Michael gets trance possessed, I get trance possessed. We work together in trance possession even when he is in America. If Michael has problems in the United States, I can sense it from this far. I think of him immediately and feel depressed. When we talk on the phone, I find out he is having problems.

Before we met there was a missing element in both of our lives. He had to be initiated by my spirits, and I also had to be initiated by Michael's spirits. When we met and initiated one another, for the two of us, the initiation was complete, and this missing element disappeared. We were then cemented as *mapatya*. We find it difficult to separate. Now I can say we complete each other constantly.

When I look at twinship, I look at the twinship between all ancestors, black and white ancestors being the children of God. Twinship creates permanent friendship. When I look in the face of my white twin, I know the rule of colonialism and racism is over.

Let us look at the ancestors: the Zulu ancestors, the Shona ancestors, the Bushmen ancestors. They all come with the same message, that we are one people, and we all worship one God. They believe and know they were created by God in his image. If we follow that principle, there will be peace today. But we have created divisions and multiple groupings that don't see eye to eye at all. We are confining ourselves into holding cells. We are unfree. There are walls around every home. What are we afraid of—our neighbor? There is no twinship there.

Some people go to Israel to pray. Fine. My people go under a big tree. Does it matter where one goes to pray? It is what comes from inside our hearts. My heart, my behavior, is God's temple. If I give myself up to my God, I give myself up to my ancestors totally and openly. In this way I am creating twinship here; one world united by my actions, not by what I say with my mouth.

If my spirits are your spirits, and your spirits are my spirits, there is nothing more to say. What I've learned from this twinship is very broad. The question is: "Augustine, how do you treat your neighbors be they black or white?" What does Europe do to their neighbor Africa? What does Africa do to their neighbor America? And so forth.

This is the way of Grandmother Spider. This is how she makes a web to support the peacemakers. She says, "To complete a true initiation, one has to be initiated by different people. And the different people must also be initiated by other people as well." Michael was not initiated by one person. He was initiated by many people. I was not initiated by Michael alone but by many other people as well. I was recently initiated by the Bushmen. They had a dream that I was going to be initiated by them. Simakuhle also had a dream that I was to be initiated by the Bushmen. This is twinship in the broadest sense.

This is the desire of the ancestors. They say, "If you become one family, you will solve many problems." If we create twinship in this way, we would not be creating weapons of war. What for? To kill my neighbor?

We can also make twinship with the earth. We can also make twinship with the animals, with the birds. Look at what we are doing to the earth today. It is a dumping place for our poisons. Some nuclear weapons are hidden in the earth. The water and the air are polluted. No wonder we have so many diseases today. They were not sent by God or our ancestors. We are making those diseases ourselves.

We do not own the land; the land owns us. We do not own the universe; the universe owns us. We do not own God or the ancestors; they own us. It is as simple as that. So we must make twinship between these things.

St. Peter was told by Jesus, "If you want to follow me, leave everything behind you and come after me." That was a particular incident that one, a particular call from God. For most people the demand is not so great. It is simply a matter of realizing who you are and where you came from.

My way, the same as with Michael and Simakuhle, was like that of St. Peter's and "now, not later," is what God said. I tried to escape, but I couldn't and was taken deeper and deeper into the circle of God's presence until I had only one response: "Here I am." One response and one responsibility—to heal.

There was no longer one obstacle I could put between me and this experience of "Here I am." Nothing at all. That is when initiation occurs, when there is no other place to go; just this place. Initiation through different people creates this twinship. The twinship is with God and everything and not just between Michael and Augustine.

Augustine Kandemwa

1
AUGUSTINE'S STORY
I JUST THOUGHT IT WAS THE WAY THINGS WERE

When I started to know about life, I didn't know that I had problems in the way I was growing. I just thought it was the way things were.

This story I heard from my mother. When my umbilical cord was cut, I became very ill. A trance medium came through the village, and the spirit said through her, "Take this child out of the village and make him a shelter in the bush. Don't give him any medication. Just take him into the bush and sit quietly with him, and he will heal."

So they took me into the bush and made a little shelter from branches. My mother nursed me in this little shelter for three weeks. She was the only one allowed to be there with me. When we returned to the village together, I was healed.

I first heard this story two years ago when my wife, Simakuhle, was asking my mother about my life. She wanted to know why I was always sick. Sometimes I'm well, the next few days I'm in bed, and I'm not feeling well at all. You know, the spirits come heavily on me at times. Very heavily indeed. I feel like I want to sleep all the time. I don't like to eat anything at all. That worries Simakuhle a lot because she knows a little bit about my life from our marriage. But my mother knows me since my birth.

My mother also told me about my father's death. He died at the hands of witches when I was young; so I don't remember him at all.

He was working in Bulawayo, my father, when I was born. He was building a round house, and some neighbors invited him to have some beer. But in the beer there were some dangerous herbs, and he started complaining of stomach problems, and he swelled up like a watermelon.

These witches took the cup away from him and got rid of it before anyone could know.

After a time people went to report this to the police in Chivo town. There were no buses back then so someone had to go by bicycle, but when the police came, my father had already died. His whole body was swollen, and he was black like charcoal. A postmortem was carried out. He was destroyed inside. His intestines were in pieces.

That is how my father died. Why did they kill him? I don't know. But in that particular community, almost no one was working, and he was. Perhaps that is why they killed him.

When I was the age of, maybe, five years old, I liked to make things with wood and stone. One day I took an axe and was working on a piece of wood and cut myself on my finger. I was bleeding profoundly.

My mother was in Harare looking for some work so she could support my brother and myself. So it was left to my grandmother to carry me to the hospital about fifty kilometers from where we lived—on her back! The nurses who were there told her to dress the wound herself. This is the way they were trained—no kindness, no mercy. "You have come to us with your sick child. That's your problem. You dress the wound. You wash it." As old as she was, there was no respect for her.

She would take me twice a week, and then she was tired; so it would be only once a week. And the wounded finger was getting worse. I was told she decided to use the herbs from the bush to heal this wound because I was at the point of death. With the herbs the wound healed, finally.

During those very, very early years, I hated *ngangas*. I didn't want to be near them. I thought they were witches. They would frighten me. I just didn't go along with them at all. When they were dancing to appease the spirits, I would say, "Get out of the place!" As young as I was, I used to think that there must be one God who looks after all. So why these dances, this trance possession, which looks very frightening?

When people would take snuff, *bute*, I would not want to sit next to them. These healing ceremonies meant nothing to me at all, and yet I loved to help the wounded and the sick.

I was a boy who grew up afraid to see people fighting, to see any form of violence. I would try to say, "Why can't you stop immediately." I remember one time when I was in very early school, and children came around me, trying to make me fight with another person. I'd just look at them and start crying. I remember this well. And one time I went to primer school outside Harare, and the bigger boys came around me, saying, "You're an excellent athlete. You run so well. But why do you do it? Why do you do it around here? We're going to beat you tomorrow. When you're in the field, we're going to get you."

So they started pushing me around. This bigger boy came with the other boys, and he slapped me on the face. What came over me that time, I don't know, because I just found him lying on the floor, and I was in tears. I was shivering and shaking, and somebody said, "You hit him." Well, I was just in tears. I wasn't happy really to see a violent situation.

That's the way these ancestor spirits work, you see. They wanted me to be a healer and a peacemaker even when I was a child, but I didn't know that yet. Becoming a *nganga* for me was a long, hard path.

2

MICHAEL'S STORY
OF SUCH SMALL THINGS
THE KINGDOM OF HEAVEN IS MADE

Ah, yes, my story, how I became a *nganga*. Well the truth of the matter is the story begins somewhat before my birth because that was when I first met you. Before I came to Africa to be initiated, I went to an astrologer in Los Angeles. In Zimbabwe he would be called a *nganga*. He is someone who understands the poetry of the stars. I asked him under what sign was the dark of the moon before my parents made love to conceive me. I wanted to find the pathway to the realm of the ancestors, and for some reason I thought this information might help me.

The dark of the moon before my conception was, on one hand, close to the summer solstice, the brightest day of the year. However there was a full eclipse of the sun. So the moon was dark that night, and the sun was black during the day, both under the sign of the warrior twins. "I don't know what this means," he said, "except that you are going to Africa to meet your twin brother."

The moon was nearly full the night I was conceived, or so my mother tells me. I like beginning my story like this. There is a happiness I feel when I think of my parents enjoying one another and a freedom in remembering that once I did not exist. I am reminded that Jesus said the Kingdom of Heaven is like a tiny mustard seed. The moment of my parent's pleasure, the planting of the seed, the gift of this life from its beginning to its end—of such small things, Jesus would say, the Kingdom of Heaven is made.

I was born in the spring of 1957, the first of four brothers with two older sisters. After I was born, like you, I was very, very sick. I got a staph infection in my navel, and I was hospitalized because of it. To cure me, they gave me a drug, a drug that they didn't know I was extremely allergic too. My mother had a priest come to say the last rites for me because they didn't think I would live.

The infection in my navel and the horror of the violence of how I came into the world put a kind of terror and rage and hunger in my body that I've lived with for most of my life—in fact lived with until I was initiated by you, Augustine. As a child, I would have nightmares about it, remembering being a baby. When I was seven years old, I would put a knife to my gut, and I would dare myself to stick it in. When I became a teenager, sexual feelings were especially terrifying. Often it seemed as if having a body was itself unbearable.

That was in the Southwest of the United States, in New Mexico, where both my parents are from, my father, a white man, my mother, a Mexican woman. The Mexican people are a mixed breed of Native American and the Spanish people who came and conquered that part of the world about four hundred years ago; so my mother's people are brown-skinned people. However, when it comes to skin color, I am certainly a white man.

From the time I was a child, my race has not made a whole lot of sense to me because at home I was Mexican while my father's family was racist. His mother remarried a member of the Ku Klux Klan, which is a white supremacist group that hates black people, Mexicans, and others. I grew up with little connection with my white family.

When I was a child, my race would change twice a day. At home, I would be Mexican; but when I was out on the street, they beat me up for being white. In New Mexico when you're a half-breed, you're called "coyote"—that's a wild dog which they say changes shape wherever he goes.

The funny thing is, now that I'm with my African family, I still change shape everywhere I go. In Zimbabwe, because I'm a mixed breed, legally I'm called "colored." When I walk on the street, however, I am white; when I am with my African family, I'm Shona and Ndebele; and when I work as a *nganga*, I usually sing in the Yoruba language, or Navajo or Spanish or Hebrew or Japanese or whatever little bits of other languages I know how to pray in. All of my life I've changed shapes. That's been what my life has been about.

3

CURLED UP LIKE A CHICKEN FOOT

One time—I think I was probably under ten years of age—my uncle was hit by a lightening bolt, and his hand was curled up like a chicken foot. My elder aunt was there with her daughter, crying, looking at my uncle. He was lying there, and they couldn't do anything. So I went into the bush and brought some fiber from a tree and tied it with a stick like a splint, opening his hand and fingers, tying the stick up to his elbow. After two days it healed. He was able to spread his fingers. That was my first experience as a healer. As you ask me, I can now remember it, but at that time, it probably meant nothing to me. My uncle was also a healer. Though I didn't like *ngangas*, my uncle was different. I trusted him.

I am told that when I was very young, he did some work on me. I have cuts on my body which he did. My family showed me them when I was grown up. Why the spirits in him did it, he didn't know—but he was told by the spirits to do it for me. So the first initiation that was done in my lifetime was done by my uncle.

Now that my uncle is dead, he is the one who comes to me when I am in trouble, and he says, "We are with you. Why should you worry?" I see him clearly in my visions. He talks to me.

When he was still living, he had personal problems with me at times, but truly speaking, he loved me so much. He treated me like his own brother. We'd play games, and he'd chase me around in the home, playing like little kids. And whatever food that was served to him, he would not eat it alone but would call me to him so we would eat together.

When somebody dies when they are young, I see them change and mature in my dreams. It seems like there is a purification that is done when they are dead. There is a difference to how they behaved when they were living to how they approach you now that they are dead.

As a spirit, my uncle fully understands me—what I am and what I'm carrying. That is why he comes in a mature way, a supportive way to show me the path. As a spirit he is wise and mature and gives me wisdom.

4
THE STRANGER
GOD HAD GIVEN ME TO LOVE

My mother is Catholic, and my father was a Buddhist. He grew up in a strict Southern Baptist family that was oppressive. When he was thirteen years old, he saw an advertisement in a comic book about the Theosophists and the Mysteries of the East. So he wrote away for their material, and he became Alamogordo, New Mexico's first Buddhist. First and only, I think.

So I was raised between two spiritual traditions. For my first years I practiced Catholicism, then I started practicing Buddhism. For a while I practiced both. In many respects I think I still practice both.

However, for about eight months when I was fourteen, I became a born again Christian, a Pentecostal. We were living in Michigan then, near Detroit where my mother was going to school. I was converted by a black preacher named Brother Bogel who had a radio show coming out of Detroit.

I was walking past a black church one day, and it was full of singing and clapping, so I shyly went in and was greeted with enthusiasm. They were baptizing a girl in a white dress, a schoolmate of mine. She was radiant. For a long time after that, even after I stopped being a Christian, every fiber of me longed to be baptized. But there was something else in me, very stubborn, that refused. If I look back and try to understand it, I think I knew I wasn't ready to give my life to God completely like that. I hadn't tasted life yet. I didn't really know what this life was about, and I felt Christianity was keeping me from finding out.

Something happened when I was a Pentecostal, however, that completely changed my life. Your story about tending to your uncle when he was struck by lightening reminded me of it.

I was adopted as something of a spiritual son by a Methodist minister named Reverend Brown, and one day he gave me a *Bible* and asked me to go witness to a fellow named George who was living in a cheap hotel. Fresh from the gutter, George was a drunk who was drying out and trying to put his life into order.

While I was reading scripture to George, he toppled over and started convulsing on the floor, shaking his head and slobbering. I had never seen an epileptic seizure before and don't even think I knew what one was. I ran off in a panic to get a couple of friends who lived nearby to help me with this situation. But they weren't at home!

When I returned to George's room, he was gone. I looked around and soon saw him walking along a busy street a couple of blocks away. I went to him, and while I walked with him, it was quickly clear that he didn't know who I was or where he was going. All he remembered was that his name was George and that he was once in the Navy. I persuaded him to return with me to the hotel.

For two or three hours I was able to encourage memory and then personality to come forth, bit by bit. After a while he even remembered who I was. What I remember most from that day was the luminosity of the light of late afternoon and the easy tenderness that I felt towards this stranger whom God had given me to love.

That evening I went to a prayer meeting and told my story, and the circle prayed over me. A woman was taken by the Holy Spirit—in Africa we would say trance possessed—and prophesied that the gift of healing had come upon me, that I was to be a healer.

This prayer meeting was the beginning of the end of my life as a Christian. For years I thought I was the butt of one of God's jokes. I remember being on a city bus and looking on a blind man across the aisle from me and feeling tormented. I knew that if I truly had faith, I could and would lay hands on him and he would see. Everywhere I went, I would see people around me afflicted in one way or another, and each was living testimony to my lack of faith, to how endlessly afraid I was.

In retrospect, of course, I'm not so unkind with myself. It seems that the spirit of the gift is always looking for an open window, and my meeting with George presented just such an opportunity. It was then that I stepped onto the path of healing, and the fourteen year old can be forgiven for not having a clue about the consequences or meaning of being a vessel for such a spirit.

5

THE LION TOTEM

All tribes—I've even discovered this is true of white people—have some totems. We have the *mvumbwe* totem, which is the Zimbabwe bird totem. We have the zebra totem. We have the buffalo totem. We've got the cow totem, the fish totem. My family totem, all the generations through the father were *shumba*—lion. A little *shumba* was born in me. When I get trance possessed, I see the lion roaring in me, and I behave like a lion.

We identify ourselves by our totem. Different people are scattered all over Africa. So when they say "I am a *shumba*," I know this is my relative. When we meet a stranger, one of the first things we ask, "What totem are you?" When a number of us lions are together, everything softens up, and we are one family immediately.

The spirits that are upon me also are one family because they are allowed to be on me by the lion. The *shumba* invites them and welcomes them. No other spirits can come through our family without the permission of the *shumba* ancestors.

The lion is at the beginning of my people, and through *shumba* we connect to other tribes and people of different races. My ancestors can welcome anybody because there is nothing above the lion. The first man of my tribe assumed the lion totem. I don't know how exactly the idea of having totems among people originated, but I understand my people chose the lion as the totem. But I am trance possessed by other animal spirits as well: the white eagle, and the spider woman, for example.

Our ancestors worshipped God. They did not have churches or temples. They used to go to particular trees like the chikata tree, which is a fruit tree. Different groups of people would go to different trees. Our ancestors believed that God lived everywhere; so some went under these trees to worship. When they offered their prayers for rain, they would have the rain.

Our ancestors knew they were created by God—by Mwari—so they worshipped him. We ask our ancestors to take our prayers to Mwari because they are so close to him. That link cannot be broken because Mwari gives us everything we have.

When the *Bible* says, "Honor your parents," it does not say the living parents or the dead parents. It just says honor your mother and father. We also go to the grave site of our ancestors. We know there is a soul in that grave.

When God created things, he said let me create man and woman in my image. Those are our ancestors, and their ancestor was God; so there is a direct link all the way back. It is critical for us to keep this chain unbroken so that we are without obstacles between us and God. God's law is very clear: Honor your parents and honor me. This is also the way someone like myself returns through Christianity back to the way of the ancestors—through the parents. Right now I believe Adam was my ancestor, Abraham was my ancestor, Eve was my ancestor.

6

THE LANGUAGE OF BIRDS

When I was a little boy, I loved God so much. Some boys want to grow up and be cowboys or astronauts. I wanted to grow up to be St. Francis of Assisi. And I was very close to animals, especially the birds and the insects. My best friend and I started a bird-watching society when I was ten years old. We decided when we got out of high school that we would get a sailboat and go to the Indian Ocean to see if the Dodo bird was really extinct like they said it was. All we cared about was birds. The other kids called us "the bird brains."

Everybody in my school knew that I was interested in birds, and a girl who I thought was pretty told me there was an owl in her backyard. After school we walked up and down an alleyway behind her house, looking for the owl but with no luck. Just then I heard the screech of a blue jay and recognized the bird's distress call. I knew the owl was farther up the alleyway; the blue jay was screaming at it. I was right—there was the owl in a walnut tree. I was so proud I could understand the language of the birds. That was one of the best moments of my childhood.

My parents divorced when I was eleven. For the few years after that, my mother, my three brothers, and I would move every year. By the time I dropped out of high school, I had gone to eight different schools. My mother was trying to get an education so she could support us. We were poor, and for a couple of years we lived in my grandparents' basement. I left my white childhood behind and moved in with my Mexican family, and all the rules changed. For a white boy a child's life is about playing. In my Mexican childhood we worked on my grandfather's ranch. On the ranch there were apple trees and maize fields. We worked all the time. On the one hand, I loved working on the ranch; and on the other, I hated it because I felt my childhood was stolen from me. I felt that I was seen not with affection but as a worker; another pair of hands to work the fields. It took me probably twenty years not to feel bitter about that—twenty years for me to forgive my grandfather.

After my parent's divorce, my father started drinking beer and liquor, and eventually he drank himself to death. It took him eight years to do it. It was hard for him to be divorced, and he felt such sadness for the world that all he could do was drink. He was fifty-two years old when he died.

During those eight years I lived away from him most of the time, but we became very close. When I was fifteen years old, he taught me how to do the Buddhist meditation which he had always done. He was my first spiritual teacher. I soaked in his wisdom as I watched him kill himself. I cried about his death for years. I was just beginning to know him when he died.

7
DIFFERENT HOMES, DIFFERENT PEOPLE

So many people cared for me. Different homes, different people altogether, not because they really loved me but because as human beings, they couldn't throw me out of their village. Somehow these people had to look after me because I was almost like an orphan at that time. Year after year it was this relative saying, "I want that child here;" this parent saying, "I want that child there." Whoever had some work to be done would say, "I want that boy for a year."

From year to year to year, I was looking for some form of education. I was wandering from this village to the next village. I was very motivated. I don't know where this came from, but I just loved being educated. Unfortunately, I couldn't get the best education that I wanted. I would hardly spend two years at one school. The type of instruction that I got was very poor, from those who were willing to offer their services—for free—to such people as I was.

I was always on the move. Luckily, wherever each school was that I went to, I would find someone who was willing to take me for a year. I went even into the little African farm schools where I could offer my services working the fields. They, in turn, would look after me, give me food, and a home to stay in. I do not know how old I was. I could have been nine or ten years old because I knew what I was doing the way a young child does not.

The British government, when it was in power in this country, set the standards for education. First there was Substandard A for every child starting school. Usually one goes into Substandard A at age seven, but some started school older than that, especially in the rural schools during the European era. Then you went on to Substandard B, then Standard 3,

Standard 4, and so up to Standard 6. After that you start Form 1 and continue to Form 6 and then university. For me it was almost impossible to get to Standard 6 level. But I wanted to go further with my education. I wanted so much to go even to the university.

By our custom my father's brother should have looked out after me through my life. He would be my second father. Once when I was visiting my mother near Harare, I met my uncle. He was a businessman with a fleet of lorries. He said he was going to care for me.

What I wanted was to go to school, but when he saw me, he thought to himself, "Oh, yes. I have got another man who can work here for me." I worked for him, yes, but when he saw I wasn't interested in business at all, he helped me find my way to Highfield Community School.

Highfield was formed by the Nationalists. Robert Mugabe, the first president of this country, was very much involved in the opening of this school back then. The Nationalists had actually seen the terrible plight young people were in because of the oppression of African people by the whites who ruled the country at that time. The whites tried really not to build more schools for Africans. What they wanted was cheap labor on their farms and in the factories and so forth. This was the situation.

At that particular time, the Nationalist parties, ZANU and ZAPU, were legal, but the children of the Nationalists were not allowed in the government schools because the whites thought they would influence the other children. When the Nationalists saw this, they decided to form community schools. The government allowed this because they believed we would for sure get a poor education and go nowhere at all. But the Nationalists hired teachers from outside of the country. We even had British teachers, American teachers. White people for that matter.

Highfield was a legal institution under apartheid, but it was under a difficult situation. The politicians had been fighting for the school. Most of the teachers who taught us were Nationalists themselves who offered their help to the young people. There were, oh, so many children, boys and girls. I remember there were seven classes of Form 1 which were operating under trees. A group of children under that tree and under that tree over there and under that tree with the teachers writing on slabs. It was difficult, but we enjoyed it because we got what we wanted.

When I completed my Form 2, I applied to some neighboring countries to get a better education and got accepted at a school in Uganda, but the government would not allow the students from Highfield to get placed anywhere outside this country. When the government became aware that there were some very intelligent young men and girls that came from Highfield Community School, they decided to seal us off. Soldiers were ordered to surround the whole school, and they placed tattoos on our forearms to make sure that wherever we went, we were recognized. We couldn't go to Harare, couldn't go outside this country—in fact, we couldn't go outside Highfield. We had to stay in Highfield under very high security and couldn't leave for any reason. Wherever we went under apartheid, we had to produce identification cards. But if we were from Highfield, we'd have to show our forearm, and we'd be asked, "Why are you here at this place? You are supposed to be at Highfield." Then they would pick us up, put us in a big truck, send us back.

Highfield students were not allowed any education after Form 6. We were not allowed to go to any college outside Harare; so I had to sneak into these colleges outside the capital. Around then I got an opportunity to take a course on teaching children at a college in the Mutoko area. I went there with friends, but we had to be careful because the police were looking for us. Fortunately, the principal of this college was a Nationalist himself. He understood our plight. "Whatever comes," he said, "I am ready for it."

At this school I was very much involved in Boy Scouting. We trained the boys to rely upon themselves when they were in the bush and to look after the old people in local homes. These were my services to the people. I was also involved in theater where I acted as Joseph in the birth of Jesus. Later I acted as Pilate in the Crucifixion. We produced two records from those two dramas, and they sold well in this country.

Still I wasn't inspired by the education I was getting. I wanted to go even further, but getting the fee to go to this particular school was difficult. Money for uniforms! During vacations I continued working at the college for certain teachers so I could get money.

I was learning to teach children, and in my second year, I was chosen to be the head boy of the whole college by the staff. I was beginning to gain a reputation of being quite good at teaching the little ones.

After completing a year as a student teacher, I was transferred to another school to teach. The following year I was transferred to another school and yet another. They were saying, "You have got the ability to develop schools. You can develop a very poor school into a better school;

so we'd rather change you from one school to another. We want your ideas to be shared." They used to toss me from one school to another with my ideas.

If education at a school was poor, I'd ask how could we better it? How could we make use of extra time to be with the schoolchildren and give them more education? Why can't we have afternoon sessions to actually continue teaching these children? Why couldn't we offer them more visual aids so they could see how things develop naturally? Sometimes I'd look at the way staff meetings were treated by the headmaster and see that he was dictating to the teachers what to do. I'd say, "Why can't we share ideas?" We'd make use of everyone's ideas and come up with a sound education. This is what my spirits led me to do and say.

8

THE BEGGAR AT THE CROSSROADS

The turning point in my life that eventually brought me to Africa happened when I was thirteen. I was gathering purple flowers not far from our house. An old Mexican woman told me they were good for stomach aches. As I was picking them, I saw a black hobo walk up the railroad tracks to where they crossed a road. At the crossroads he saw me and walked over. He shook my hand, and he said, "I'm very hungry. Could you feed me? I haven't eaten for a while. I'd be much obliged if you gave me some food."

This was a part of the United States you rarely saw a black person; lots of Native Americans, lots of Mexicans but really no blacks. I think my little brothers were frightened; they didn't know what to make of this stranger I brought home. I boiled two hot dogs and made him a hot dog and ketchup sandwich. This was my feast for this beggar.

Before he ate anything, he prayed for about five minutes. He blessed the food; he blessed me; he blessed my path in the world. And then he ate. As he left I gave him little candy bars called, "Space Food Sticks." The package said the astronauts took them to the moon so they would have enough protein. After I gave him the Space Food Sticks, I watched him walk off into the desert. He was going from Kentucky to California to live with his family: all the way across the United States. It's probably about five thousand kilometers.

This man changed my life. Completely. Twenty years later I was to meet him again in rather a different fashion. When I was studying the Yoruba religion, a West African tradition from Nigeria, I understood that this was the spirit they call Eshu Elegba. He's the spirit of the cross-roads, and he opens the gates to the Mysteries. When you treat a beggar kindly, miracles can happen. He opened the gates. He gave wings to my feet. Two years later I was the vagrant.

For five years I did nothing but hitchhike all over the United States, Canada, Mexico, Guatemala—over a large portion of North America. I would either hitchhike, or I'd jump freight trains and ride with the vegetables. When I was sixteen years old I hitchhiked from Southern California to Alaska. The last two thousand five hundred kilometers was a gravel road going towards the North Pole. When I got to Anchorage, Alaska, I found a mission that gave food to down and out Eskimos. I had breakfast with them, and then I hitchhiked across Canada to Newfoundland, which is as far east as you can get in North America. For years, this was my passion.

When I wasn't hitchhiking, I lived on the street. I was homeless for three years between the time I was seventeen and twenty years old in a small town in California. There were basically two things that led me to be homeless. But the truth is nowadays when somebody asks me why I was homeless, I usually say, "Well, you have to get an education somehow, don't you?"

The first thing that sent me to the street was the President, Richard Nixon. America was at war in Vietnam. I was involved with Catholics who were against the war. During Christmas of 1972, Nixon decided to bomb Vietnam into the Stone Age. This is the time in America when you hear Christmas carols about peace in the world everywhere, and the President decided to viciously bomb the Vietnamese people.

At that point I said, "This is not my country. I love the people in this country; I love the land of this country. But this is not my country anymore." Americans were involved in killing three million peasants in Vietnam. I knew that until we grieved about that, I would be an exile in my own country. That's when I became homeless.

The other thing was that I wanted to be like St. Francis, a beggar saint. The funny thing is, of course, on the street you get corrupted quite quickly. I became a skilled thief to steal food. I rarely begged. It was too humiliating. There was plenty of food to get out of garbage cans, and I was very good at collecting wild food from the bush.

It's hard to describe being on the street. I'll tell a sad story and a humorous one.

The sad story—I was hungry one night, and I came to a bar that was playing music. There were people waiting in line on the sidewalk in front of the bar to buy tickets. Somebody had spilled a whole bunch of pistachio nuts. I love pistachios. I looked at the people, and I asked myself, "Do I have the courage to get on my knees in front of these people and pick up these pistachios so I can eat?" I prayed about it and then got on my knees, pretended like nobody existed but myself, and put the nuts in my pocket. I walked on, but at first I felt so nauseous I couldn't eat them.

The funny story is about another time I was also hungry. I had a great idea where I could get food. I lived by the ocean, and there was a pier where the fishermen would sell fish. I figured that at the end of the day, if they thought the fish was too old, they would throw it away. So I went to the pier to an Italian fish salesman, and I told him that I had a cat and I wondered if he had some old fish I could feed it. He was delighted. He said he had three cats of his own, and he asked me all about my cat. I didn't know anything about cats; so I started making up stories about the kind of cat I had. And while I was telling him about my cat, he swept fish guts off the floor of his stall, and he gave me a big plastic bag full of them. "They love this stuff," he said. I thanked him, and I took my fish guts with me, feeling happy and ridiculous.

On the street I spent most of my time in a university library studying. I had dropped out of school, but I was hungry for knowledge. My days were made up of getting food from the garbage cans or wherever, spending some time with friends and going to the university to study anything that I wanted: poetry, world cultures, plants, philosophy, psychology—you know, anything. I was so interested in all of it, I just soaked it all up. I knew that I was preparing myself for my life. The truth is I was preparing myself to be a *nganga* because all I wanted to do was heal the world. One way or another all my studies revolved around that desire.

The second year I was on the street, I lost my mind; my life was so painful, and I could hear the spirits calling for me. I think I went crazy because I needed to be with them. That's in fact what happened. I met an ancestor, an old man who wears animals skins. He was one of the many spirits who kept me company during that time. Being crazy was not hard though I was sometimes frightened. I called my father on the phone, and I told him, "I'm out of my mind. I'm seeing spirits everywhere."

He replied, "It's okay. When I was your age, I went through the same thing. It's a rite of passage. This is your initiation. You can trust it."

Those were the kindest words anybody had ever spoken to me. I knew after that I could trust the spirits; I was no longer afraid of them.

After I went crazy, life became difficult. The spirits had come, and then they abandoned me. I was left in the dust. Fifteen years, I think—I felt like I was eating ashes every day for breakfast, lunch, and dinner. There were other good things going on, but nonetheless, I tasted ash in my mouth all the time.

I moved to San Francisco in 1975. There the garbage cans didn't have food. I had nothing to eat. I had dysentery for a few months and would wake up every morning soaked in my own diarrhea.

I tried to prostitute myself, but at that time there were parasites under my skin and I was always scratching. I had open sores on my body, and nobody wanted to have sex with me. I suppose there's some bleak humor in this. I went to the Gates of Hell and asked admission so I could sell myself as meat at a reasonable price. And those in Hell, who are always hungry, turned me down because the meat was spoiled. As it turned out this was during the time that AIDS was percolating in San Francisco. Those little bugs under my skin saved my life. I've always been grateful to them for that.

It got pretty bad. What happened ultimately is that I began feeling invaded by everybody's eyes. When you're homeless, you know that you're an object of disgust; you sense you're an object of fear and everybody's eyes pierce through you. People who pity you, people who want to help you, people who hate you—you're dealing with it all the time. You feel naked. You feel like you have no skin.

When I was at the very bottom, all dust and rags, a couple of times a week I would pass a woman on the street who worked in a local book shop. She would smile at me and say, "Good morning," as if I were a human. That was the beginning, the middle, and the end of the story.

I knew better than to pursue even a friendship with this woman. I didn't want to frighten her. But that smile, that "Good morning" was the single thread that kept me from falling into the abyss for the last year I was homeless.

Twenty years later, I did a public reading in her bookstore of my first book, and I thanked her. Of course, she didn't remember this casual act of kindness, but I think about it almost every day. Through this story I came to believe that no act of kindness is insignificant. There is no telling its value to the other person or what might come of it.

All this time I felt called to go to the forest and spend a year alone there. It was then I was healed by the water spirits though I didn't know them by name. I went to the coast of Big Sur in California and off into the woods. I carried in food, books to write in, books to read, candles—everything I needed for a whole year, though I actually only lasted one month. During that month I prayed and tried to understand how I had come into such misery. Every day I would go into the river and say, "Wash away this history. Forgive me. Bring me back to myself." During my time in the forest, I began to see my ordeal as a pilgrimage to the essential story that would live in my bones the rest of my life.

This time alone was the first time I saw myself as an old man. I was only nineteen, and I was shocked that a boy could have an old man's spirit in him. I didn't know it was possible. The old man seemed to understand the sad and true meaning of my story of homelessness. The old man told me that soul is made up of such stories, but when I asked, "What is this thing you call soul?" he didn't answer. It occurred to me then for the first time that young as I was, I was not yet ready to understand the meaning of my life.

9

WORDS TO TALK ABOUT GOD

I think that because I'm talking about my education, I should talk about Christianity. I am not a Christian, but it was the churches that gave me words to talk about God.

The schools I went to practiced Christianity. The first school that I went to when I was perhaps seven years old had been a British Methodist Church school, but I didn't go to church. Church at that time meant nothing to me at all. I didn't know the difference between being a member of the church or not being a member of the church. It was all the same. It was just a matter of playing games with other children while the old people were at their church service.

Later it was the Anglicans. They taught us what it meant to baptize, what it meant to repent and so forth. If you are not baptized, you are an evil person. This is what they would say to young boys and girls. I remember very well when they tried to baptize me in the Anglican Church. I was at a mission school in the Chivu area.

At this particular mission we would cook our own food and get our own water from the river. So the young boys and girls went into the woods to collect some firewood to prepare the food before this particular day of baptism.

I was told that someone had seen me walking with a girl collecting firewood. I said, "Yes. That is very true. We were collecting some firewood." I was told that they didn't want me to walk with the opposite sex. Walking with the opposite sex meant nothing to me. It was no different than walking with a boy. They said it was in one of the Commandments. I said, "Well, maybe I don't know about this Commandment. My intention was to gather firewood, that is all."

They said, "You cannot be baptized now." It was a big issue.

Some of my teachers came to intervene, saying, "This young man could not have done anything like that. This is a lie. Somebody must have created a lie here because we know him."

After all this they decided I could be baptized, and the headmaster came to me and said, "I see in my vision that I must give you a name, but I cannot tell you it until the day of your baptism."

When I went into the water, the headmaster was at my side, and the priest asked, "What is his name now?" And my teacher said, "I want him to be called Augustine." That's how I got this name. Before that I was called Alexander.

When I came now into my secondary education, I went into an American Methodist Church Mission where I was taught by American missionaries. But I knew if I did not follow what the missionaries wanted, they might try to find out more about my background. If they found that I had been taught by Nationalists, they would chase me away from their school. I had to be careful.

It was here that I came to love church, especially when they talked about God the creator, how we could serve Him. I immediately began teaching Sunday school. We were given bicycles to cycle to local villages to entertain the young little boys and girls. I loved to do that! Ah, I enjoyed that work very much! Even during the cold season, I would say, "I want to go and meet those boys and girls!" Right out there in the local bush, in the surrounding farms.

I began to sense that there is a creator above all, God Almighty. I'd look at the preachers and try to understand whether they knew what they were talking about. I began to see in my inner head that some of these preachers really were preaching so that they would be respected by the local people and that they didn't really know much about God. Still I was convinced that God was there. I stayed even though I did not believe in those religions—Methodist, Anglican, what-what and so forth. I believed in the God that they were praying to but not the religions themselves. This is my relation to church.

10

THE BLACK LIBERATION ARMY

After I left the forest, I was still committed to changing the world. At that time the police in the small town I lived in were trying to acquire machine guns to repress those remnants of the antiwar movement they felt were subversive. The police were becoming like a military unit, which was not right. I became involved in an effort to keep machine guns out of the hands of the local police.

I had read the autobiography of Malcolm X when I was in the forest, and I was convinced that the revolution was in prison and that I had to connect with black prisoners. I started working with the Black Panthers both in and out of prison. They ran a free food program in the ghetto to feed the children and old folks. I'd bring them wild mushrooms and go to supermarkets where they throw out fruits and vegetables that were a little old or cheese that you just had to cut off a little mold. I'd go to the fields outside of town and gather artichokes and onions that were left behind after harvest. By then I was an expert at gathering food from every possible source. When you've been hungry, you learn to be an expert in gleaning and gathering.

At the same time I made connections with the Black Liberation Army. These were prisoners who wanted to make revolution in the United States. At that time such people were, without a question, very—what's the word?—"macho" is the word we say in Spanish. They were confused men who believed in violence to solve things, and they were also self-destructive. I'd visit them in prison. I'd smuggle drugs for them to sell to other prisoners to pay for legal fees.

When I was in the BLA, we were organizing a small guerilla army to go to Rhodesia and fight in the War of Independence there. We were in contact with a woman in the Italian Communist party in Italy who had connections in Africa. We were going to be trained in weapons in southern Italy by the Palestinian Liberation Organization and then go to Rhodesia to fight apartheid.

I was the only white person amongst them. Needless-to-say this was not a good thing. They treated me very poorly. It was confusing because they also depended on me and regarded me as a friend. But it was not a good scene at all. Ultimately it came down to watching my friends destroy themselves for three years.

One good friend left prison after eight years. In prison he was like Buddha. Nick was so calm and so smart, so sharp. The week he got out of prison, he was selling drugs on the street and carrying weapons. After four months I lost contact with him. He was driven to either get back into prison as quickly as he could or get himself killed. Those were the only choices he knew. He couldn't stand being on the outside.

This was my first connection with Rhodesia. The irony has not escaped me that I did not come to Zimbabwe as a warrior. I didn't come to fight. I have come to make peace, yet it took me twenty years to get here.

11
WAR

Remember, all of this was happening during the time of war when we were trying to free this country. In the early sixties the youth were active politically, especially in Harare and Highfield. I was one of the organizers in the Nationalist movement that was involved with mobilizing the youth so that to some extent we could force some whites to recognize that an African was a human being. At that time a young man of my age would say, "You say baas to me," just because he was white. When I worked for my uncle, I would take trucks to go and buy firewood from farms that were owned by whites. The attitude that I saw on these white faces... We would be taught, "Don't touch that gate there, you black man. Wait for me to say whether you can come in or not." Or the white person would never care to talk to you, but he would tell his gardener, a black person, to come and say, "What do you want?" We'd speak to this white man through his gardener or through his cook.

The Nationalists were saying during that time, "I think that we've talked to the white people for a long, long time, and they don't want to listen." I can remember one Nationalist saying, "It's time to collect stones and throw them. This is the only language that white people understand."

There were many demonstrations in support of the Nationalists who were being arrested, but we were told that if we took part in any demonstration, we would be shot. We were told to keep quiet and shut up. If we reacted, they would shoot right away.

I saw this with my own eyes in Highfield. Seven blacks were shot dead while I was looking. Just like that. One by one. The next one. The next one. (Snapping of fingers.) They were covered in red blankets. In front of me! In a school yard, you know, on open ground. One by one.

(Snapping of fingers.) And oh, yes, with children around and parents. Shot dead in my own Highfield. I won't forget that one. It is still there in my mind.

I saw one man who was shot in the leg. The leg was in pieces. My uncle was there sitting with me. I stood up and went straight to this man to help him. I dragged him into our yard, and my uncle said, "The police are going to kill us."

I said, "It's better that they kill every one of us." I won't forget this.

I tied the leg to support it and stopped a taxi. It was illegal for anyone to stop a taxi to carry someone who was injured in this war, but I did, and I dragged the man into the taxi and said, "Please, driver, take this man to the hospital right now." And he did, for free.

My uncle was rather dissatisfied with what I was doing. He was not happy at all. I was going to get us into deep problems with the police and the government. But nothing bad happened at all in our home. I was involved in rather a secret something now going on.

You know, the only weapons we could use in Highfield were stones. What else could we use? The whites had every weapon at their disposal, not to shoot animals but blacks. We used road blocks. This was the 1960s, the 70s and so forth, before independence in 1980.

We'd set road blocks along major roads. If the police were going to detain the Nationalists, why not detain the police? All the roads in Highfield, all the roads in Harare with barricades and so forth, drums, broken bottles—putting them on the road so we could protect the Nationalists. We knew that if these leaders were taken away from us, we would be helpless. We went on a rampage and destroyed the street lights so the police could not identify the homes of the Nationalists. But I was more interested in helping the injured during the operations. I liked doing it. That was my major task, really. I wanted to take care of the suffering people.

Every family in the country was touched by the insurrection. Even now as a *nganga*, I tend to the spirits that were wounded during those years. Even my own mother. I remember during this liberation war my mother came to see me. She was living in the Mangaron area near Mozambique. I advised my mother not to go back home during that day or the following day. I felt in my heart that something bad would happen, but she insisted.

She went by way of open truck because busses were not operating in those areas where the war was very hot. The truck hit a land mine and killed almost everybody, including the driver. My mother was thrown some meters away from the explosion, and her legs were broken. I was told that security forces carried her by helicopter to Harare Hospital. The security forces came across this piece of paper with my name and phoned the school where I was working so I would know what had happened. That is how I was informed.

12
BECOMING A NURSE

I fell in love with my first wife when I was doing political organizing. Marsha was a kind, Jewish woman; a political activist; a feminist. I moved off the street to live with her. After having been with Marsha for three months, my father died, and then my daughter, Nicole, was conceived two months after that.

It was terrifying to live in a house. It had been years. I don't know how to describe it. I felt confined and suffocated.

Marsha had a college degree. She worked as a schoolteacher. Financially it made sense for me to stay at home with Nicole. I became the "mother" in the family. Loving my daughter and being at home with her was an opportunity to recover from my time as a street kid.

Marsha was—is—a good mother, a very good mother. But I was a boy who had been homeless for years, and I was terrified of her. I certainly was not a good husband. I was a good father, but as a husband I had affairs with other women. I made my ex-wife suffer quite a lot, and she ended up leaving me after seven years for someone else, a friend to whom I had introduced her.

After Marsha left me, I was devastated. For seven years I had a home. Though it was strange to live within the four walls of a house, nonetheless, I had a roof over my head and food to eat. I had failed everything. I really wanted to be a good husband, but I didn't know how. I was not capable.

I did not go to my father's funeral. I couldn't bear the sadness I felt. And I was ashamed to cry in front of my brothers and sisters and my mother.

But my shame and grief left me hollow inside and unfinished; so I started doing volunteer work with people who were dying, and I found that I liked it a lot. The first part of my training as a *nganga* was on the street. The second part was working with people who were dying, mostly people with cancer; later on, people with AIDS and other diseases. During that period I had assisted with my daughter's birth and was asked to help with a couple of other births as well. This was an incredibly rich time for me. I felt honored to be a part of these passages; birth and death. It changed me. I decided to train as a registered nurse.

13
BECOMING A POLICEMAN

All this was happening—the war, my discovery of God and beginning to teach children—when I came back down to Harare on holiday. During this time when I was living with my uncle, he introduced me to a friend who was in charge of a certain police station in Harare. That officer wanted to find a qualified schoolteacher because he was going to open a police school. I didn't want to be part of the police force because of my politics. I just didn't want this at all having been in Highfield under police occupation. But my uncle's friend called a secret meeting to make me to join the force without me knowing it. The police force was integrated, but whites wouldn't let their children go to school with black children. They wanted me to teach the children of black policemen.

This policeman friend of my uncle's asked me to take a letter for him to a recruitment officer in Harare. "Please, my son, can you deliver this letter for me?" I said I would do it, not knowing that I was carrying a letter that had something to do with me. I took it to the recruitment office, and they just looked at me. They didn't want to interview me because they knew I would refuse to join them.

They listened to me, treated me as a friend, and I listened to them and so forth. They had already sent a letter to the Minister of Education saying they had found a qualified teacher. They had sent letters to my previous schools asking for recommendations. "How is he?" and so forth. I couldn't warn my schools in time to say bad things about me. My transfer by the Ministry of Education into the police force was granted without my knowing it. I was accepted into the British South African Police, the BSAP. When I looked at this letter from the Ministry of Education, I thought, "My God, what on earth is this now?"

I stopped teaching while they trained me. The training was long and tough. I had to know the law. Everything. When I completed my training, they sent me off to teach. So I found myself teaching in a police uniform. I didn't like it, but what could I do.

Under those conditions I decided to go and visit some of my friends in Highfield who were Nationalists, members of the National Democratic Party, ZAPU, ZANU, and so forth. I consulted with them, and they said, "Well, if we are fighting this government, we are lucky because we've got you in the BSAP. You'll learn a lot about how they operate." This is how I started. I was happy to see how the British South African Police Force operated.

One time the black officers had our annual meeting with the senior white police officer. We were to be addressed by our bosses, the whites, about the conditions of service in the British South African Police. One guy, a black man, stood up and requested information about our pension fund. This boss stood up, angry and bitter, and began to show his true colors, saying, "You blacks don't ask that question. You are not policemen. We are only training you to be our messengers."

In response to such insults, we were trained to say, "Yes, suh!" Whether you agreed with him or not, it was just, "Yes, suh!"

That moment awakened me to the situation we were in. When we were given some forms to complete, I took them home and tore them to pieces. I didn't want any part of this.

But I was forced to join. A few months later after this incident, another white boss who was younger—I could have called him my brother —came to the school where I was. He wanted to search all of my headmaster's professional books. Just because he was white, he had to look at everything the blacks were doing. But this was not his school at all. He knew nothing about what we were doing there. He acted as if he had the right, as if he were an official from the Ministry of Education. Not just anybody in the British South African Police could inspect my headmaster's books.

I greeted him like a friend when he came into my office, and he just started looking at what we were doing in the classrooms. I showed him everything. Then he said he wanted to see my records.

I said, "What records?"

He didn't know them by name. He said, "You keep some records here. I want to see them!" I said, "Mr. Heatherly, you cannot do that."

He said, "Why?"

I said, "You don't have the right to look at these documents here. The only people who have the right to do that are from the Ministry of Education. You can only come to see whether the buildings are in good condition. That is as far as I know about your duty."

He insisted that he was my boss, and he sat on my chair, saying, "I am your boss, and you will do whatever I say."

Then I started talking to him, and I said, "You know, you are my brother, and I welcomed you here. I know you are my boss because of your color, but just because of your color. Yet when it comes to this place, you have gone too far. I am saying that you are no longer my boss in this room."

He became angry, very cross. "I can put you in jail for saying that," he said. "Putting me in jail doesn't solve the problem. It will even make things worse between you and me." "Don't talk to me like that, you *kaffir*."

"That's enough, sir. I'm closing my office. You can go and talk to your senior officer, or you can take me to prison right now. Lead my way. I will go," I said.

He said he was going to report me to his boss. He went to the police administration and stayed there the whole day. The following morning he came back and said, "Augustine, please forgive me." The next morning! "Please forgive me."

I said simply, "Thank you, brother."

So that's one of the incidents in a long life, a long journey through life. I'll never forget that one.

I don't hate the white man, really. I hated the system, that evil system. I prayed in those days that such a system would come to an end peacefully.

When the British South Africa Police sold my services to the schoolchildren, they decided that I should teach two classes operating from the same classroom, one group facing this way, one group facing that way, and I did that for several years and for no extra pay. They called them good services from a poorly educated schoolteacher. I don't really know how good these services were. Yet I enjoyed being with these kids all the time. I wasn't married. I'd even approach their parents and say, "Can I have them in the evening? I'll teach them for free!" Because we were living in a police camp, the children were often at home doing nothing. So I'd ask teach them in the evening from seven o'clock to half past eight.

14
THE SWEETEST OF GIFTS

My daughter and I moved into a little shack. It didn't have any running water; it had no bathroom. It had a light and a tin roof. I started to get food out of garbage cans for the two of us like I did when I was homeless. But eventually I worked my way through nursing school. I got my degree.

I started meditating a lot. In the ashes of the divorce, I realized the only thing to do was to give myself over to learning to love. That's the only thing that matters; the only thing that has meaning in the long run. I practiced the Buddhist meditation of my father, and I learned to eventually find a calm heart, to the degree that I was capable then. Life began to make sense. I wrote a poem to the person who my wife left me for. "The kiss of betrayal was the sweetest of gifts," I wrote. Had Marsha not left me, I could never have entrusted myself to the spirits like I did. After nursing school I got all of my friends and my mother and family together and shaved my head. My mother and my brother Paul and my daughter all cut off a little hair, and then I cut the rest and shaved my head clean. After a night of drunkenness and laughter, I went into the woods the next morning for three months of solitude to meditate and pray. I spent time watching the animals and learning to be silent. I learned what silence was for the first time. I didn't know how to live in silence, but I heard silence.

The old grandfather spirit I met when I was nineteen returned—the one in my body who was so weary. We became acquainted. I realized he was not me but someday in the far future I would ripen into him. This time he wasn't as weary as before, and he taught me many things. I learned that there was a laughter beneath the bottom of despair. During my twenties and thirties, I spent about two years alone in the forest. Every time I returned, my friendship with "the old man" deepened.

When I came out of the woods, I got my first job as a nurse. I didn't want to get a job. I wanted to stay in the woods forever. I worked at the bedside of an old woman with multiple sclerosis. She had a hole in her neck so she could breathe with the help of a machine and had been in bed for thirty years. She couldn't talk, but I learned to read her lips. We became good friends.

I worked from eleven o'clock at night until seven-thirty in the morning. Usually when I came to work, I'd say hello to her and talk a little bit. Then I'd kiss her and put her to sleep. All night long for six and a half years I was able to meditate and pray. That was a gift of the ancestors, a great gift. In this life I don't think I'll ever have enough time to meditate like that again.

The first few months of meditating at her bedside stripped away a Catholic hallucination. Looking at her in the dead of night, sound asleep with the nonstop sound of the ventilator filling the room, I imagined I was looking at the anguish of the Crucifixion. Beyond that I thought that it was mine to identify with that anguish, to meet it with whatever dark and hidden suffering I had within me and maybe become a saint in the process. Then one night, reading lips and expressing a few hardly audible words through her vocal cords as I plugged the hole in her neck with my thumb, she asked me how I was.

"Oh, a little sad I suppose," I said.

"Why?"

"Nothing really. Life just seems sad to me sometimes."

"I rarely feel sad," Mildred replied.

"How is that, Mildred? Some people would feel quite bitter if they were in your position."

"I just don't let things worry me, that's all."

It was true. Seeing Mildred as Christ on Calvary was just the product of a hyperactive imagination of a never-to-be again Catholic. It was sufficient to be gentle in turning Mildred in her bed, in cleaning her up after she had used her bedpan, and to tell her how beautiful she was.

15

I STARTED HAVING POWERFUL DREAMS

Let me talk now about becoming a healer. In 1978 or 1979 I started having very powerful dreams. I could not understand them because I never dreamt like that. Before he was President of this country, His Excellency, Robert Mugabe, would come to me in dreams. He and Joshua Nkomo, who became Vice President, would visit. They would say, "We want to show you greater things," and they would take me to Great Zimbabwe. "You see this place here in the cave; it was used by the fighters hundreds of years ago. Do you see this place here in the cave? It was used by elders who made the decisions. Do you see this place? It was used by our spirit mediums." Mugabe and Nkomo showed me all these holy places. This dream came to me many times.

I used to tell my relatives about these dreams. They could not interpret them. I was left wondering about what they meant.

Later on at the end of 1979, near Independence, I'd see myself flying like a white eagle, overseeing what was happening. I would be given messages for Mr. Mugabe about how he must look after the older people of this country, the sick, the suffering, if he wants to rule. But I was scared to go and tell Mugabe about them.

Sometimes answers to problems that had been worrying my family about how we should do things for our dead people would come to me in dreams, and I would tell my relatives. They would say, "Yes, I know that is a problem," but they didn't know how to go about addressing it until I told them. My relatives began to question where I was getting these dreams from and what was happening to me. I would tell them, "I don't even know."

The dreams even came when I was working with the BSAP. They were vivid dreams telling of the Ministry of Education officials coming to inspect the school and the books, that they wanted more this and this and this, and I'd tell the headmaster about that.

At one point I went to tell my headmaster that he'd better check some important records in the school because an education official was coming to have a look at that particular set. "They are suspecting that you are not using that set correctly."

The following morning at eight o'clock a man from the Ministry was there. My headmaster said to me, "Young man, I must tell you there are powerful ancestors working on you. You had better find somebody to initiate you."

Aha! He started a war with that. I said he must never, ever talk about ancestors working on me, No! No! But he insisted. "I don't believe in ancestor spirits!" I said. "They don't mean anything to me. I believe in the Creator who created the ancestors. This is my road. I believe in the Creator, the controller of the Universe, not the spirits you are talking about. No."

So he said to me, "Each time you get dreams about me, let me know because they help me a lot."

I said, "No problem. I'll do it." But I started having dreams that his wife was going out with other men. I didn't tell him that.

I was a Christian, a strong believer in the church, so I wondered why I was getting these dreams. I felt miserable in my life then. I didn't know what to do. But then came a time I wanted to be baptized in a particular church, the Worldwide Church of God. The leader was a Mr. Armstrong of the United States. This man tried baptizing me in the Meikels Hotel swimming pool in Harare, but my spirits resisted. These spirits who brought me dreams wouldn't let him push my head beneath the water. The moment he touched my head, it was difficult. He asked me if I had repented completely, and I told him I had. So he said to me, "Why is it difficult to baptize you?" I said I didn't know. He tried again. It was impossible!

He said, "We'll try it tomorrow."

When I came back to my home on a Saturday morning, he followed me to my place. He said, "Augustine, it is better you stop from coming to this church yet for a reason I don't know."

I agreed with him. After this I stopped going to churches.

16
THE PICTURE OF BEAUTY

Let me say a few words about my second wife, Deena, and my daughter, Nicole. Deena is the one that's going to be with me until I see her off to the grave. We have a deal between us—she gets to die first. She doesn't want to bury me. So that's the way we're going to do it. She's twenty years older than me, so the chances are that's the way it will go.

When I was still married to my first wife, I had a dream about making love with a woman who was much older than me. I was just twenty-three years old. I told a friend this dream, and he smiled. "Well, I suppose you will have to do that someday, won't you?" I felt at that point that the ancestors wanted me to be with a woman who was older.

I had been meditating for five years at the bedside of my patient, and it was time to bring the part of me that's a monk together with the part of me that loves women. I wanted to see if there was a way in which sexuality and spirituality could be compatible and together. Deena wrote a wonderful article about that called, "Revamping the World." She's a feminist writer, a poet, a novelist, a thinker, and a fine healer.

I wrote a twenty-eight page letter in response to her article. The article itself was only a few pages long. I decided I was going to court her with my intelligence. Of course, she didn't know me at all, but at the end of my letter, I wrote, "P. S., I think the two of us should be lovers."

I didn't know that Deena had spent a year and a half of her life being stalked by a man. I did not know the violence she had suffered at the hands of men. A stranger writing her a letter saying maybe she should be his lover was not something she was excited about. She says she thought I was probably an axe murderer, at best.

I was patient. I knew we were supposed to be together. A year later we finally met through a mutual friend and got along quite well. We had breakfast together, a little coffee, and I said, "You know, in my deepest heart, I think you and I should be together." This was our first meeting.

And she said, "Well, that seems more possible now that I've met you, but your letter really frightened me."

In spite of the shaky start, we fell in love. She was writing a novel called, *What Dinah Thought*, about Israel, about Jews and Palestinians, and she gave me the manuscript before it was published.

I wrote her a two hundred page letter in response to it. Turning over every little sentence, I told her how the words revealed her soul. Of course, she fell in love with me. I was relentless.

We've been together for fourteen years now. Aside from being twenty years older than me, she is one breasted. She lost a breast to cancer. When I first met her, she was frightened that I would not find her beautiful. But the truth is she is the picture of beauty to me. She is the picture of beauty. I love her so much. She is such a good teacher and friend.

Nicole is also the picture of beauty, also a good teacher and a friend. She is now older than I was when she was born. Incomprehensible! And she is such an adult—tough minded, soft hearted, and gorgeous.

I was a child when she was born; a rather frightened child if I tell the truth. Layer by layer, answering what it seemed her spirits called for, I learned to be a man and an adult. Her gift! That someone such as I would become a man.

Nicole is an actor and a director. That is her passion and her vocation. Sometimes I laugh with her, tell her that it's in her blood. When she was born, I was such a wreck of a human being, I thought it was most sensible to read books on acting so I could puzzle out the role of being a reasonably good father. And now here I am, a *nganga* of the theater of the spirits!

A few weeks before I first came to Africa to be initiated, I went with Nicole to Santa Cruz Island off the coast of California. It was time for her to leave home for college, and so the two of us stood at the crossroads in our lives. Of course I wanted to extend the father's blessings to the gift that she is, but I also felt compelled to confess my concerns that I might have wounded her when she was a little girl, growing up as she did alongside a father who was thrown here and there by his spirits.

Our first night on the island, she read to me what she had written that day in her diary. I remember the words exactly.

"My dad seems to think he was a bad father. All I can think to say to him is, 'Here I am.'"

She is such a teacher and a friend. Sometimes when I'm taken by narrowness or hardness of heart, Nicole quietly reminds me of the values I raised her by, and I remember to keep faith with them.

17
WATER SPIRIT DISEASE

One day my mother said, "When you come home, could you buy me some *bute*?"

I said, "Mother, I don't handle *bute*. I don't like it because snuff is associated with ancestors. I'd rather give you the money, and you go and buy the *bute* yourself."

My brother who had a job in Harare had all sorts of ancestor spirits working on him. I'd take him to *ngangas* and say, "If you want for this man to initiate you, I will pay for it. You go in the house, but I will not go in. I'll stay outside, and you can do your own thing. And when they come outside to pour beer for the spirits, I will say, 'Please excuse me.'"

For years I resisted the ancestors. Then one year I had a problem with my knee. I couldn't stand up. I couldn't stretch it. A dislocation, they said, but where? I went to the doctor, and he said, "There is nothing wrong."

I said, "Look, I'm feeling terrible. I can't walk!" X-rays showed nothing, and then my right elbow started hurting too. The headmaster came to me again, and he said, "Young man, I told you, these are your ancestors. These are your spirits."

I said, "God created two things. Life and Death. I'm prepared to take either of the two. If this thing is going to kill me, I'll take it that way." That's the answer I gave him. I now know that the knee pain was a message that I should submit to my spirits, but my thinking was, "Instead of visiting a *nganga*, I would rather die."

This went on for some time. My headmaster used to send a driver to collect me because I couldn't walk. Then I developed a flu, a strange flu.

I went to see my doctor. He gave me what he gave me, the medicines of the hospital. They never worked.

Around this time I saw my face in a dream. I was dressed in a police uniform with *bute* in my hand. Yes! In the dream I said, "Never! Not *bute*! I'll never take that. If this flu is going to block my nose and kill me, that's okay because I'm still prepared to die."

An old woman from the village—I didn't even know her—came to me and said, "My son, you are suffering from the flu."

I said, "Yes."

"You've got problems with your knee."

I said, "Yes."

"You've got problems with your elbows."

I said, "Yes."

"I want you to take this snuff when you go to bed. Just take a little bit. I'm going."

And that's it. I took that snuff, just a little bit of it, and the flu was gone, immediately. When the spirits wanted some more, I'd take a little bit. That's how I started taking *bute*. That resistance—gone!

So...I started taking *bute*, and that released my pain, but something new developed. When I was sitting in my office during my day at work from eight o'clock in the morning to about twelve o'clock noon, I started feeling as if I had to go to bed. I would sleep in my chair and start to dream, seeing various shapes and colors which I did not understand. Some of the visions really frightened me. I saw huge, wild animals, big birds, and sea monsters all the time. I asked myself, "Is this because I'm now taking *bute*?" There was no answer.

This happened for quite some time, every working day for months. At twelve o'clock I'd lock up myself in the office so that no visitors could come in and interfere with what was happening to me. People would come and knock at the door and think no one was there.

Then one of my staff members, a female teacher at my school came to me and said, "Headmaster, I have something to talk to you about."

I said, "What is it?"

She said, "There are a lot of things I see in you. You may not believe in them. You may not accept them. But there is something that I see in you. I see that you are a sick man."

I said, "No, I am not. I'm not sick."

She said, "You have a terrible heartbeat."

That was true. It was so.

She said she wanted to take me to a medium spirit.

I resisted for three weeks, but things were getting worse for me. I definitely thought I was going to lose my job this time because I was always sleeping at work.

So we went to this woman who was a spirit medium. When she saw me, she laughed. She laughed and laughed and laughed. I was going to be cross with her. I wanted to get up and walk out of her place, but I continued sitting and watching her because she was trance possessed.

She said, "You are trying to resist the powers of the Creator."

I said, "Oh, yes."

She said, "You will never win. My young man, you are playing with fire. You will never win. You had better go do this—and that. Follow what the spirits want. That is it. You are not going to die just because Augustine says he would rather die. You are going to submit. The spirits are with you. They want to make use of you." I kept quiet, gave her some money for her services and walked out. I said to my friend, "Is this what you wanted me to hear? I'm not going to return to see her!"

I thought I was going insane. At that time I had gone through all the police ranks from the constable rank on up, through promotions and so forth. But these dreams kept coming. I would spend the whole night seeing people sitting in circles, talking to me.

Then I saw some people coming from the water saying that I shouldn't worry about these dreams. They said the dreams were coming from them. I didn't even know these people at all though some of them came in human form in the likeness of my relatives. Some were women who looked like my aunts. Others were men who looked like my uncles, but they were very old. All the time they were coming from the water, talking to me.

One member of the BSAP called to me one day. I didn't know him. He said, "Brother, can you come closer to me?"

"Good morning. How are you?" I said.

"You are taking too long with these spirits," he said.

"You are taking too long. This is the only thing I can say to you now. Bye bye."

I don't take too long to obey the spirits. I didn't respond. I resisted more. I had a car that I used to drive from home to work every morning. I decided to sell it, for no reason. I wanted to use buses like any other person. Two weeks later the car I sold was sold again. So I bought it. I used it for some time, and then I decided I wanted to sell it again. Some of these ancient spirits, the *Mhondoros*, they hate cars.

Finally I began to go down. Each month I was getting two hundred dollars, but it started to disappear bit by bit until finally I had no bank account. I couldn't work well. I'd sleep all the time and have nightmares. So I started visiting *ngangas*. I wanted to see if anyone would initiate me.

18
WHILE THE CITY BURNED

I flew into Los Angeles to be with my wife and a friend who was dying of liver cancer during the Los Angeles riots in 1992. A fellow named Rodney King, who is a black man, was pulled over in his car by four white policemen and beaten to a bloody pulp. This is not unheard of in the United States. However, this time there was somebody across the street with a video camera, and it was caught on film. The policemen were brought to trial, and the white jury, in spite of the video evidence of clear police brutality, voted the police innocent.

At that time some people in the black community rioted and started lighting the city on fire. Not only black people, Mexicans and white people also rioted. People were outraged. I flew into Los Angeles when it was burning. I couldn't get into the city. The skies were so filled with smoke, the planes couldn't land. It took my plane six hours to get there for a one-hour flight. When I finally arrived, Deena drove me directly to the house of our friend Hella, who was on the edge of death.

In the middle of the fire, in the middle of the riot, this woman had one of the most beautiful and peaceful deaths that I have ever seen. Hella died tenderly in her son's arms at two in the morning.

The next morning I walked onto the streets of the city, and there was shattered glass all over the place. I passed a black woman on the street. I could feel the distance between us. She had ash on her and apparently had been rioting. She could not look me in the eye, and I could not look her in the eye. There was a gulf between us, and it seemed as if there was no conceivable way to reach across it.

I returned to Hella's house. They had taken her body away. Our friends had poured good wine to drink, to celebrate the life of this woman who had died so well. When one of the police helicopters flew overhead, I started weeping about the world that my daughter was growing into. I wanted more than anything to know what I could do to heal this world— to heal this world, to lay hands upon it, to allow it to break my heart, to let Spirit break in, to yield to Spirit, and to find the courage to act.

19
INITIATION

I visited so many people. So many in Harare, around Harare, each one claiming that he was going to be able to initiate me. They all failed, and I was paying them money. That was how my money started disappearing, and I was left with nothing, absolutely nothing.

In 1985 I met a young man named Smart who came from Gokwe. He was an Apostolic Church member, a prophet. He saw my problems in his visions, and the spirits in him told him to tell me I shouldn't go to any of these *ngangas* to seek for help in my struggles. I asked him why, and he said, "Now I don't see anybody who can help you. You are not yet ready. But time will come, and you will see someone who will help you." I could not understand this.

One day I went to a *nganga* in Harare. He's a famous *nganga* for seeing people's problems. He said, "I see very ancient spirits on you. I'm just going to try to help you. I'll keep on calling on your spirits to help me."

I stayed with that man for two years. He tried his best. Smart came again when I was at this man's house. And he said, "Augustine, have you forgotten what I told you? How long have you been here?"

I said, "Two years."

Smart told this *nganga*, "If you help this man successfully, I will give you everything I have. I say this because I know you cannot do anything for him."

Three days after Smart had spoken to this healer, I had a dream. A voice said, "All these *ngangas* you have been with have no power to initiate you. That is why they fail. You see this old man here in front of you?"

I looked in front of me. There was an old man with a bald head. He was speaking the Ndebele language. Then the voice said, "This is the person who can initiate you. Initiation is to be done by that old man." This is the truth. That dream was the turning point in my life!

Monday morning I went to work, and a phone call came from police headquarters to say I was to transfer immediately to Matabeleland. Matabeleland is where the Ndebele live. And look at me now. I'm still here.

Three months later this old man came to my office. He was just sitting outside on a bench. He approached me very nicely and said, "How are you?" We talked a lot. "Where did you come from?"—that sort of thing. Then he said, "You know, young man, you are not well."

I said, "What do you mean?"

He explained. "You have been having very powerful dreams, dreams which you do not understand. You have been to so many *ngangas*. Am I wrong?"

I said, "Oh, no. You are right."

I never asked where he lived. I never asked his name. I had been to so many *ngangas* who were claiming they could initiate me. I thought he was one of them.

For two months I never heard from him. I failed to be initiated in Harare. I didn't want to start failing in Matabeleland too! I'd done what I could, and I decided not to worry myself. I'd just sit and wait.

Then one day a friend of mine said, "Could you accompany me to see my friend." So we went to this place and who did we find? There was that old man who had talked to me.

I was ready to admit to myself that I was sick, very sick. He started talking to me this time more profoundly, using his spiritual powers. I agreed with him.

The night before the initiation began, I saw in a dream a circle of spirits gathered in an African hut. Half of the circle was a group of old women. On the other side was a group of very old men. Some had long hair, others were bald headed, long bearded and so forth, but all of them were old. I knocked, and they said, "Come in." Next to me was my uncle who had died recently, the one who had been struck by lightening. He said, "Come and sit next to me."

I sat next to him, and he said, "You have come."

I said, "Yes."

And he said, "We are the ones who have been calling you."

I looked at them all. I knew him and his older brother. These two I knew. The rest I didn't know. He said, "We are the ones who have been calling you. We are the ones who are still calling you."

When I looked at them all, I fell down and started weeping. I wept for a long time, and when I woke up the following morning, I was in tears.

I went back to the old man and told him this dream. He started initiating me.

There is a difference between how the Shona are initiated and how the Ndebele people are initiated. The Shona like it to be done with the bringing of beer, mbira playing, drum beating, and so forth. With the Ndebele people, it's a more vigorous initiation. One dances until very tired, exhausted. One has to do physical exercises in preparation for the coming of the spirits.

The reason the Ndebele want everyone to dance is because they are warriors. Take my little boy Moses—we will take him out into the bush to dance and run and do physical exercise to be prepared for whatever might come in the form of war. The Shona were not like that. That's why we were attacked by the Ndebele. We were not physically strong at all.

You find among the Ndebele some people who have no dancing spirits. My wife has dancing spirits and spirits that don't like dancing at all. The Ndebele man who initiated me saw right away that my spirits didn't want to dance.

One thing I noticed about this type of initiation where one is to be vigorous in dancing and so forth is that it is difficult for the people with water spirits. They could not be initiated that way at all. The way I learned to deal with people with water spirits was different. They were to be initiated quietly, peacefully, and their spirits will come. They sit in this room quietly, meditating, smoking, or eating herbs and quietly go into the water to pray. Water spirits are spirits of peace, so I initiate them in a peaceful way.

He initiated me for two years. I was told in a dream that he had finished his work with me.

"Young man," he said, "you are going to be a great healer. You are going to serve a lot of people but don't be afraid. Your spirits are with you."

These were the last words he said to me.

When I reflect on that dream about being initiated by an Ndebele, it is clear that peacemaking spirits brought it to me. They wanted peace between the Shona and the Ndebele, a Shona man to be initiated by an Ndebele man.

He also had a dream that after he initiated me, he was to be initiated by me as well—by a Shona man. And when I did that, his spirits came through for the first time in him. So this was the bridge between the Shona and the Ndebele. This is what happened.

My ancestors, when they were still living on this earth, didn't like violence. They wanted peace. I was told by my own elders that they accommodated any people and cared for them. When they would see war between blacks, they would say, "What is this now? We used to live peaceably with our neighbors." Maybe the ancestors saw why there is conflict between the Shona and the Ndebele people. What caused it in the first place? This is maybe why they suggested I should be initiated by an Ndebele.

When I was going to be transferred back to Harare, the people in this community went to pray to the mountains and said, "Why do you want this man to return to Mashonaland?" They prayed hard.

Instead of being sent back to Harare, my spirits said, "No more." I'm staying in Matabeleland and not because I want to but because my spirits say so. This is a sign of reconciliation because the two sides have seen the cause of the conflicts. Now we have planted the heart that can span in all directions without divisions.

The Ndebele people, the Zulu people, the Bushmen, the Tswana of Botswana—these are my immediate relatives now. I love them, and they love me. Their spirits love me, and I also love their spirits. All these people and their spirits are saying, "Here is your home." This is Zimbabwe. Zimbabwe shouldn't have any divisions at all. What for?

I experience peacemaking through my work. I do not say, "I can make peace." The spirits make peace. With the spirits, there are no divisions.

There are spirits that work through people to divide one tribe from another. There are spirits who work through people to unite us all. It depends on what spirits you are listening to. The spirits I am listening to are the peacemakers.

The warrior spirits are there to protect the peace-loving people from the bad spirits, the *ngozi*, that influence people to fight and destroy others. The *ngozi* spirits, for example, can destroy a whole family, for the love of doing it. They just enjoy it.

The warrior spirits that are upon me fight that evil spirit to protect the community. There are so many peace-loving people in this country. Those are the people who can be protected by the warrior spirits. The warrior spirits I have myself. Yet if you attack them, they retaliate. If you don't attack, then there is peace.

When I was initiated by the Ndebele-speaking man, my spirits came to him in his dreams saying, "We are the spirits that are on Augustine." They told him before I was sent down to Matabeleland, the Shona and Ndebele spirits had had their own conference. When I arrived, the spirits had made their resolutions and were ready waiting for my initiation.

The same thing with Michael—he had a dream several years back, meeting me in Africa. That is how the *mapatya* thing started. The spirits are hungry for reconciliation between their children.

20
SO THAT THE SPIRITS CAN HAVE A HOME

I won't tell again here the story of the path that led from the riots to Victoria Falls. The visions, the terror, the sense of futility, the prophetic dreams—these things I've written about elsewhere. It is curious to me that I naturally look at my water spirit illness as a breaking down of structures so that the spirit can have a home. You speak of water spirit illness as the stubborn resistance before finally giving in. Yet the story is the same. The spirits long for a way into the world, and as you've said to me many times, it is such an honor to serve them.

It was at Victoria Falls, weeping in each other's arms, that we stepped into the mystery of *mapatya*—these strange twins who come from such different worlds and yet the same world. It has been a few years now, and I continue to watch layer after layer of this mystery reveal itself. The way I speak of it to Deena is that you and I are joined at the root, nourished by the same rich soil.

First, of course, there is the matter of biography and temperament, the endless small and large coincidences. I remember how we laughed when we found out that both of us almost died as babies because of having infections in our navels; moving around all the time as children, that rootlessness of so many schools, towns, friends; the death of our fathers that shaped us so and set each of us yearning for the ancestors; you working for your uncle, me for my grandfather; the hatred of violence, and with it being terrorized by those for whom violence is a form of pleasure; the hunger to learn and from a young age both of us engineering our own education; the passage through Christianity, its gift of a language to speak of God; both of us honoring Christ, rejecting the religion, grateful for the gift; both of us incurably plural in our spiritual lives; so many spirits, so many languages to sing of the sacred.

Both of us were politicized as adolescents: you under apartheid, me in the shadow of Vietnam and American racism. Both of us stood close to those who confronted oppression with violence and civil disobedience, and both of us chose the path of the peacemaker and healer.

The peacemaker and healer—for you and I, Augustine, these are two faces of the same spirit, and my deepest bond with you as *mapatya* is our camaraderie in the work of healing and peacemaking. Like you, I married a woman of the "other" tribe and have tried to understand what it means to be bonded to someone who comes out of a world that, over the centuries, my people have tried to annihilate. And after the bloody riots in Los Angeles, my dreams led me to be initiated by you.

In your case your spirits led you to marry an Ndebele woman, and your dreams led you directly to your initiation by a *nganga* of that tribe though so many thousands of Ndebele have died at the hands of the Shona in recent years. Once you told me of leaving a snuff container on the grave of an Ndebele king as an offering, and I'm reminded of the rituals of prayer and peacemaking Deena and I performed at the death camps of Eastern Europe a number of years ago. Such spirits that lead us in this way know that peacemaking is healing and healing is peacemaking. They know that there is no teacher more profound than the one who bears the face of the "enemy." And they certainly know that healing the human village and healing the individual is the same work.

I could go on and on, *mapatya*. During my first initiation with you, I said, "It seems as if our spirits are beginning to get acquainted." Your response was, "Oh, no. They have always known each other." These twinned spirits clearly knew each other long before we met. It was they who drew us together across time and space so that we could meet in this unbearable time and perform their rituals of mutual initiation. That such a thing is possible—our meeting, our friendship, this mutuality—will never cease to astonish me. The world is really quite vast once one steps out of the tight little grid of colonialism and racism.

My third initiation and the months that followed made it possible for me to completely embrace the life of being a *nganga*.

You and I and Deena and the Canadian healer Patricia Langer made a pilgrimage to the ruins of Great Zimbabwe, and you showed us those secret and holy places there that had been revealed to you in your dreams.

One such place was the cave where the Shona kings were buried. High up on a hill, it overlooked the maize fields below, the little villages with their round houses and thatched roofs, the surrounding forest.

Patricia, who has an eye for reading the patterns of energy in places, was able to see the passageway between the worlds where the King's spirit returned to the realm of the ancestors, and she was able to instruct us in how to sit on his throne among the rocks and how to give over to his death.

Sitting on the King's throne and looking down over the fields and villages, I was soon filled with a radical sense of benevolence and power, solid and assured. Through the King's eyes I knew I lived for the fertility of the land, the welfare of the people and the animals, and nothing in me was distracted from serving their interests. Without knowing it until that moment, I never knew what benevolent male power was. I never really knew it existed—the world being tortured in all the familiar ways by tyrants and charlatans. Male benevolence I knew. But to be fully empowered without arrogance for the welfare of others was another thing altogether. It was sufficient to glimpse it, to know of its possibility, to know that the King resided in my flesh.

When I laid down to draw the King's last breath, the ground gave way into a field of white. First there were presences receiving me, white wings opening up and softening the passage, but then it was simply free fall into endless space. No bottom to touch, just falling, forever.

When I left the cave, I was able to rejoin the human world, I suppose. Indeed, the following two weeks we were involved with the challenges of initiating a group of people. But in fact, this free fall lasted for several months.

For the first three months, it was as if I were back in the bitter days of water spirit illness: the emotional disorientation, the vivid dreams and hallucinations, the exasperated and hopeless recognition of the depth of my suffering and the suffering of the world. Oddly, however, the hospital and the work of the healer became my sanctuary. It's easy to become mindlessly involved with one's own pain until you are with people who are facing far worse, and facing it often with far more grace. In practicing kindness, I felt sane.

21

THE COMING OF THE SPIRITS

My initiation by this Ndebele man, this "so-called" enemy, was a blessing in disguise. I was being taken to my true home in Bulawayo among the Ndebele people. The first few years that I was a *nganga*, I continued to be in the police force and continued to teach. I was placed under difficult conditions. We had white police commanders who were so harsh to the black policemen. This pained me a lot. I was always praying all people in Rhodesia would someday unite and be one people. When my dream told me that I was to be initiated by an Ndebele man, I thought how am I going to live in Bulawayo amongst the Ndebele people, given the enmity between the Ndebele and the Shona? It was terrible for me at the time to come down to Bulawayo. How was I going to control the staff at this new school where the majority were Ndebele people? It was difficult for me.

Definitely for sure, when I got here, the staff was divided. The Shona would have their tea in their room, and the Ndebele on their own. But when I went to this school, I simply listened to their problems. I talked to them in a fatherly way, and to my surprise, eventually we were having tea in one staff room. I came to the Ndebele-speaking people with the question of how we should develop the school. That seemed to heal the divisiveness. When I left that place, there was true unity. I was received with warm hands by the Ndebele people. In some ways, more than anything, my police work with the Ndebele prepared me to be initiated by an Ndebele man.

Soon after initiation, I started dreaming that I was sitting on the edge of a big river looking into the water. In a moment different types of herbs came floating on the water so that I would look at them and admire them fully. I would call them in the dream, "my flowers." The whole night they would appear like that; different types.

Among my flowers I would see a woman who looked like a fish. The herbs were like hair, long hair. She asked me, "Are these your flowers?"

And I said, "Yes."

"Go and collect them. Collect them from the river and bring them to your home," she told me.

The first three days I had this dream, I'd say, "What are these flowers here?" because I didn't like to handle any flowers at all. The dreams kept coming. I went to a river near where I was living and picked a few, just a few and took them home.

The mermaid came again in a dream and said, "We are not learning to heal. We were born healers. I want more of those herbs." My own spirits were coming to talk to me after the initiation. "We were created healers. We are great healers. Go and get our herbs. Prepare these herbs this way, this way, this way." So I started doing it.

Then an old man came, but he had wings. He lived in the forest, alone. He was busy boiling some herbs in clay pots. Some of his herbs were drying on rocks and others were already powdered. He was pounding some herbs, preparing them. I went to his place accompanied by this mermaid and watched him. This old man never talked to me. He only talked to the mermaid, and I didn't understand what they talked about.

The old man came to me again in the next dream to show me other herbs, not from the water this time but from mountains and forests. He said, "These are my herbs. I am a great healer."

That mermaid is the one I call Ambuya—Grandmother—Chop-chop because she is fast, efficient, that one. She owns the herbs in the water and along rivers and lakes. The old man is an earth spirit. His are the herbs of the forest and the mountains. The two of them taught me how to mix the herbs so that my medicine has the power of water and earth. They came to show me that I was to be a *nganga* who uses herbs. I was surprised by this.

This is how I started collecting herbs. The spirits showed me how to use them, when to use them, how to prepare them. This is the way of my spirits. They are doing it the way they like. This is how I became a healer. It is not through training by anybody. I became a healer after initiation the way the spirits wanted.

22
SLOWLY AND WITH GREAT TENDERNESS

Buddhists say that compassion is born in the charnel ground, the field where hope and fear have been reduced to ash. During those three months, suffering within, suffering without—life was just a gaping wound. And yet I was stubbornly committed to a mad project. I thought if I dug deep enough into the fact of suffering—mine, my patients', the world's—then somehow it would make sense. I was heroically seeking meaning, any meaning, but was constantly left with Job's lament. Then one afternoon as I was sleeping off my night shift, a spirit came to me in a dream.

He was a raggedy beggar, perhaps a little drunk. He shouted just a few inches from my face, "You have got it all wrong, all wrong. Stop this search for meaning. You will never find it, and if you do, you will never be able to convince yourself of what you find. When you look at the suffering, just remember you are looking at your face in the mirror. There is no meaning to it at all." Was this clear! The hospital then became a hall of mirrors, a sacred place of meeting myself.

That night I returned to the bedside of a patient, an immensely fat black woman afflicted with a kind of flesh-eating bacteria. No one knew how to stop it, and she had two large, infected wounds, one in her buttocks that I could stick my fist into and another smaller wound in her groin, quite close to her vagina. Of course, keeping feces out of her wounds was not easy. The doctors wanted to cut into her abdomen to make a colostomy. She refused.

Twice a shift I'd inject morphine sulfate into her IV line, and after it began taking effect, I'd start the elaborate dressing change. The wounds were packed with gauze soaked in salt water, and pulling the gauze out had to be done slowly and with great tenderness. Then I would change gloves to remain sterile and repack the wound with clean gauze.

It was 5:00 a.m., and the television was on above her bed. It seems they were selling some cream that removed scars. "I'll have to get some of that," she said, and we laughed. Then came an evangelist named Creflow Dollar, who assured us that believing in Jesus would solve all financial problems, and we both agreed we should get some of this Jesus fellow also. This woman was a classy lady, and I asked her how it was that she was able to keep her sense of humor intact, given what she was facing.

"Oh, I don't know," she said. "I guess I'm just a silly person."

Ever since the spirit came and told me to drop my heroic effort to make sense out of it all, my work as a healer has opened up and at moments is translucent. It seems sufficient to "do unto others as you would have them do unto you."

23
INDEPENDENCE

The ancestors were involved in winning our freedom. Without them apartheid would be with us to this day.

During the second Chimurenga war, my brother actually wanted to go and join the freedom fighters. He traveled from Harare to Mt. Darwin, far east near the Mozambican border where my mother's relatives live. When he got there, my uncle took him to see the guerillas.

In order for a young cadre to join the liberation struggle, he had to see a medium spirit. The guerillas took him to the spirit, and she said he must not fight because he had a spirit that fought the whites in the last century. He was to operate internally, spiritually, so the spirit in him could guide those fighters out in the bush. He asked the spirit medium what would happen if he joined the guerillas, and she said, "You and these men will be shot." And so they sent him back to Harare.

When my brother was off in the bush with the liberation forces, I didn't know where he was. I went to his wife, and she didn't know either. This touched my heart a lot. I prayed hard all week.

During that week my father came to me in a dream. He was sitting on a big rock, smiling at me. "Where is your brother?" he said. "If you had come together with your brother, I would tell you many things. Go and find him!" Then he disappeared.

My brother came back, of course, but that was the first and only time I ever saw my father.

I had actually lived under that colonialism since my birth. So the coming of Independence in 1980 was the birth of new life coming into this part of the world. We wondered in the beginning are we really going to experience true political independence? The whites had reigned for a hundred years. Was it possible that an African could take over and bring us true peace? At first I thought the whites were trapping the blacks. I thought that when the Freedom Fighters came out of the bush, the whites would get hold of them under the pretext that there was to be independence and majority rule. I watched this situation carefully, but it came. Independence came! The liberation was real. Freedom was there. We were allowed to go into white owned shops now. We were allowed to move around freely on the streets which where there were white families. But still I thought, "This can't last. This is going to change someday. Look at how uncomfortable the whites are when they ride a bus with blacks on it!"

In the police force you would see white police officers talking to blacks for the first time as if they were their friends, but we tried to resist their wanting to come and unite with us. We really saw some changes in the police force. I could even take snuff at work, which was a thing never heard of under colonial rule. Being a healer, being a *nganga*, working under this new government, was entirely different because before it was considered evil to do the healing spiritually, following the ancestors. Under apartheid we could play mbira only in our own homes as it was considered evil. You had to do it privately. If you were detected, that was the end of your career. You could not remain a member of the police force. The one thing that was considered holy was going to church because the whites knew that listening to the ancestors spelled the end to apartheid. Independence, 1980, brought the freedom for me to maneuver and do my work with the spirits. After independence I could operate from the police camp as a *nganga*. I had free reign, very free reign. People would come to me, and I would help them.

At first I actually didn't want to show people that I was a healer, but people just sensed it. I started seeing things in people's faces. I started seeing their problems and the causes by just looking at a person. This went on for a long time. When I told them their problems, they agreed with me one hundred percent. "That is very correct," they would say. They were surprised how I could see their problems in their faces like that. And I was even surprised myself because I didn't know what was happening in my life. That is how I started healing people with the water spirits. The spirits themselves would say to me in my dreams, "We know how to deal with these people."

The first woman I actually helped was a woman who used to live here in Bulawayo, in the township. This woman had a dream fifteen years ago about me. So finally we met after my initiation. She came to my home, and she talked about her long-ago dream and her sickness. I was listening attentively. Then I started doing what my spirits were telling me to do immediately. I was afraid because I'd never done it before. I closed the door because I didn't want others to see what I was doing.

After doing three initiations, she became trance possessed, very powerfully, by seven spirits. And the seven spirits came one by one, relating how the young woman had suffered and how they had been waiting for me and how they knew about the powers of my spirits. They told me things I'd never heard of.

So that was my first patient. That woman with seven spirits. This was surprising because I'd never even seen it. I didn't even know how many spirits I had myself. Right up to now, I don't even know how many I have.

When I was through healing this woman, she went to tell others who had similar problems, and people started to flock to me.

When it came to healing, I was surprised because my spirits told me never to charge any fee for anybody. I received people who could have paid me for my services. I also received poor people with nothing at all but who were very sick. In a dream I was told to heal all these people. The ancestors said, "These are my people. They are suffering."

I do this work wholeheartedly and with excitement. I remember one time when a blind man was brought to my place. He had one leg amputated, and the disease was affecting his other leg. I worked on this man for two weeks. He got back his eyesight at this place here. Soon he could see everything. Soon he was able even to drive his car on his own. His other leg healed up, and he was able to use it. I did the work for nothing.

24
INTO YET ANOTHER HEART

A week before my fortieth birthday, I went off into the woods to spend four months alone. I had planned this time of solitude for almost twenty years. My daughter was grown and off to college, and my grandchildren were pulling on my soul. It was time for me to pause and digest what my life had been so I could give myself over completely to the next phase. It was time to let these years of initiations seep into my flesh. It was time to meditate and pray and come naked before God.

My old friend Jay Salter drove me down the Big Sur coast of California, and under the cover of night, we unloaded hundreds of pounds of provisions—food, candles, books, writing materials. Sharing a bottle of dark beer and a few awkward words, I separated from him and spent most of the night carrying everything to the bottom of a ravine where a small creek runs into the ocean. I love this particular place. It is where I was first restored by the water spirits after I was driven crazy by my years of homelessness. Indeed I slept in a cave alongside the very pool I did my rituals in back then.

In a place like this the old familiarity of the huge rocks which kept me company over a half a lifetime ago gave me a blunt and constant confrontation with timelessness and time; the unsolvable riddle that it was only yesterday when I was a teenager among these rocks. Still it seemed not a thing had changed, and yet nothing was at all the same. Beyond that it was clear that the remainder of my life, however long or short it would be, would pass in the seeming blinking of an eye. And another kind of timelessness too, that of living within the circle of the natural world where my life and its dreams are quite irrelevant.

For the few days before my fortieth birthday, I prepared for my death. As a *nganga* I'd often taken people through the rites of death, the perfect blend of my training in Africa and the years I practiced dying as a Vajrayana Buddhist. However peaceably I'd accommodated myself to it, I was still in free fall since that afternoon at Great Zimbabwe. It was time now to do this rite completely and without reserve so I could give myself to the strange territory between lives where the ancestors do their work; to die so young—unfinished, riven with regrets, aware of the tenacity with which I sold myself short, lied to others and most intimately to myself. I had failed at so much, and yet there was a sad and sweet recognition that I had faithfully approached every interaction with the dogged desire to learn what love was. People knew that was true of me, whatever my flaws.

The need to be honest down to the bone, to forgive and be forgiven, persisted through the first two months of my time alone. This was the closure of a life that I had to learn to love before I could pass on. In Latin this is called *amor fati*—to love one's fate. How difficult that is!

The night of my fortieth birthday, I ritualized the moment of death by offering a little snuff to the creek and climbing into the cold dark water. Afterwards I shared a cup of harsh rum with Eshu, the Yoruba trickster spirit, and imagined the shades of my friends and family celebrating a wake in the world of the living which was receding away from me.

Even after one has become a ghost of oneself, memory persists and with it heartbreak. When I was scouring my past, I acknowledged for the first time that I had raped a woman when I was homeless—a madwoman. I was shocked both by the fact of it and by the fact that I hadn't realized then what I was doing. I was thrown into the turmoil of what else I didn't know or couldn't acknowledge, especially in my relationships with women.

How could I not have known? It's strange how memories can become a way of amnesia, of not seeing the stuff of one's own life. The "official" version of my years on the street had resolved into the story of the horrors I'd survived and the laughter and cunning with which I did so. I never really forgot the woman I raped, though. She had simply been filed away among those things that I refused to look at too closely.

As a memory the incident fell under the category of "disgusting things that happened to me when I was on the street." The "to me," of course, is critical since rape is something one does to someone else. I also filed the memory under the category "sex" which was quite different from "making love" in my mind: "sex" being about the urgency of desire re-gardless of the partner, "making love" being about the sweetness of intimacy with one's partner. "Having sex" was always something confus-ing to me for all the usual reasons, but it was quite distinct from rape. Rape, I believed, was something that I couldn't do. I was, after all, known for my gentleness. And so I raped this woman not admitting I was doing so, not knowing until half a lifetime later.

I will not linger with the ugly details. I will only say that I pumped furiously trying to find pleasure but soon found myself in an empty space where neither of us seemed to exist. When I was lost in this excruciating realm, she whimpered, and I opened my eyes to look at her fear and bewilderment. "Dear God, what am I doing?" I thought. I felt nausea and dizziness spinning out of a refusal to continue.

I touched her cheek and withdrew from her body. She was afraid of the dark. The rape was complete, and I walked her back to the halfway house where she lived and returned to my cold sleeping bag on the street, exhausted and feeling dead inside.

In the woods I was to be alone with my demons in that hell where I believed that forgiveness was not possible. Yet somehow I had to yield to forgiveness. Somehow I had to find the courage to surrender to God.

I know that forgiveness would be a shallow and sentimental thing if I didn't dig down to the harshest understanding of what I had done. This was not a self-punishing gesture or even one of self-accusation. It's just that there is a blindness that could not be penetrated unless I risked see-ing myself through the eyes of my victim. Though I was never raped, there were numerous times when I was sexually violated as a homeless teenager. I went deep into those memories so that I could find empathy for what this woman had suffered at my hands.

During the first half of my hermitage, the woman I had raped and those who had done me violence were my fiercest teachers. Between them they cut through worlds of lying and self-delusion. To the exact degree that I refused to forgive those who did me violence, I refused to forgive myself for their faces were really no different than my own.

My heart collapsed into yet another heart when it finally broke into the continuous music of ocean and stream. I cried out in the dark woods, wailing through the open throat without a soul around for miles and then the solace of silence falling like a leaf. I did not know what the heart was until that moment—neither my own nor the heart in which it was enfolded. My victim and my enemies had delivered me to the true beginning of a spiritual life.

There is a heart which is not mine though it lives intimately in me. Yet it could also be said that I live in it or that it lay invisibly between all of us. Outside of this heart I could not find forgiveness. Inside of it the wine of compassion flowed freely. Inside of it I could speak the simple prayer of beginning again.

The starkness of solitude is of a piece with its beauty, and though I speak of wrestling with demons and the hard work of looking myself in the eye, it is actually the absence of drama that carries truth. My days were simple, utterly simple, and there is little that can be said about them. There is no "story" in telling of the rising and setting of the sun, the changing phases of the moon, the intimacy I found with my comrades—the wood rats and the deer mice who would share my evening meals—the passing pleasure of watching the whales swim north from their breeding ground in Mexico.

For several hours a day and into the night, I would sit on my meditation cushion, the breath coming in, the breath going out. At midday I'd pray by the stream and give myself over to the water spirits.

A couple of times a week, I'd gather bags of seaweed and spread it out on the hot stones to dry. After it was dry, I'd go through it carefully, pick out the little sea snails and limpets and return them to the sea. In this way I was able to supplement my evening meal of ramen noodles and canned beans.

There is nothing that equals the beauty of water: the braiding of the stream as it passes between rocks; the wave that swells, crests, curls over, and crashes on the shore. At sunset I'd sit where the creek enters the sea, the tide coming in and pushing against the current of the stream, salt water mixing with sweet waters. This constantly shifting boundary where the waters meet seemed to me to be the essence of holiness, and there was both gratitude and mystery in the knowledge that it might well be years, if ever again at all, before I would see it as I was seeing it then.

A refinement of prayer can happen when one is a hermit, soul seeking the right words, the true words to address God. In the last few weeks I was alone, it became clear to me that surrendering myself completely to God and surrendering to the work of healing the world were exactly the same gesture. And so in the afternoon when I would go into the creek, I would surrender to God and to the community of beings that sustains me and that I labor to sustain. "Thank you for having made of this life a gift to the world," I'd pray as I left the water, shivering.

Sometimes I was taken by the humor of the paradox that surrendering all I am without reluctance meant both "Everything" with a capital "E" but also merely this life, puny and forever awkward. Nonetheless it has its own peculiar beauty. It seemed everything and yet so much of nothing.

There is a forgivable delusion at the beginning of a long period of solitude that one is stepping from the known world of people and community, over the edge, into the wilderness that is by its nature unknown and unknowable. When I left Jay at the roadside and walked into the night at the beginning of my retreat, I was radiant with this delusion and enlivened by the terror and gravity of the moment of leaving the known world behind. What I didn't understand and could not have anticipated is that returning to the world was every bit as much a stepping into the unknown, that the world of human beings constitutes an untamed wilderness in its own right. Stepping over the edge from solitude would have its own terror and gravity, but this time without the saving fiction that the world could be divided between the known and the unknowable. Now it was all unknowable, and I was called to improvise the life of a healer within that unknowability.

Does this make any sense at all, *mapatya*? I recall a conversation I had with you once when I asked you how one tells one's own thoughts from the voices of the ancestors. "Oh, it is very difficult," you responded, "because initiation removes the you that is in you." The "me in me" was quite gone, and I knew it. Sky and stone declared it to me by day and the cold air and the stars by night. Moreover it was clear to me that a self would be created in dialogue and interaction, nothing less than actually created. It would be only a matter of days until I'd be with my beloved Deena, and the moment I'd open my mouth and enter into the incomprehensible give and take of human exchange would be the moment of being born out of the realm of the ancestors.

The preposterous improvisation of the self—to act as if I had faith when in fact I wasn't at all sure I had the capacity to have a simple conversation with my wife, much less leave the world of the ancestors for the intimacy of marriage. As it turned out, when we embraced and looked in each other's eyes, I cried like a baby and couldn't speak. As we drove north to a rented cabin, I trembled quite a lot.

As far as I recall, the only sensible thing I was able to say was that, in spite of appearances, I was not out of my mind and that she mustn't be afraid. There was a bridge to cross, and I would need her help. She assured me that I didn't seem insane to her at all. Upon hearing that I was able to draw the first breath of my new life.

Deena was impeccable—skillful and kind. Between making love and talking, I found that what I was told in the woods is true, that the self is actually born out of the mystery of dialogue and interaction. You and I know this as twins. Like us, like you and Simakuhle, Deena and I are joined at the root. I gave myself a month of re-membering and re-creating a self with Deena before reentering the complexity of practicing as a nurse and *nganga* in the hospital. I had a month of putting a little flesh on my skinny body, long walks in the woods, endless wild and fascinating conversations, lots of wine, feasting on the sacrament of marriage.

It seems that while I was in solitude, Deena had been in her own fierce passage, consciously and generously, hour by hour and day by day "giving herself away," as she put it, to the community. The parallels between her life in the community and my time alone were far from superficial; both of us walked the path of surrender. And so she needed me as much as I needed her to help cross a bridge back to intimacy.

25
I KNOW IT IN MY BODY

I came to understand why I couldn't go along with Christianity the way it was being practiced. That element of total surrender wasn't there. People can preach and talk about God or their ancestor spirits in a light way, but when I look at myself and the spirits that control my everything, the most important thing for me is to surrender totally. I can feel that these spirits are being sent by God, and they want somebody from my family to carry this work. I was chosen to be that person. So I've no option except to totally surrender my life to this. This is who I am. When I do my work as a *nganga*, I have the confidence that I am doing the work of my spirits, total confidence in them. I also know that I've got guidance from them and support from the most powerful spirit, God. I know it in my body.

In our tradition trance possession is a revelation of the place where dreams originate. These spirits are the powers that give us dreams. These are the powers that protect us, that can talk to us, which can lead and guide us. They may come in the form of trance possession to talk to the people around you. They have messages for the people around us if you are a healer as I am. Some of the things I may not know, but the spirits know about them. They come and talk to us directly. These are the spirits that tried to come when I resisted. They have the power to trance possess you, to leave you alone, to talk to you through your dreams, or even to speak to you when you're sitting like this. We have to let them come the way they want to come, either secretly or openly through trance possession.

It seems somewhere along the line with white people, trance possession was suppressed by some other power. The whites that grew up after this suppression forgot the way of their ancestors so the new generation is scared of them when they appear.

This is what I think, but I don't know because I'm not a white person. I can't speak for them. This is only my opinion.

Some of our own African people are afraid of seeing a trance possessed person. I was one of them. The whites tried to destroy the way of the ancestors; our connection to these spirits and to the Word. They tried to destroy the power that supported African people. So it is that some of our people still run away when they see a trance possessed person. And yet it was the tradition long before their fathers or their grandfathers lived. When some Africans see a trance possessed person, they think he's crazy, he's mad. That is why I tried to resist in the beginning. I didn't know.

The second time Auntie Deena came to Zimbabwe with Michael, I saw how much she needed to be connected to her father's spirit and to her ancestors. I understood that one immediately because I spent so many years looking for a *nganga* who would put my own father's spirit in my body. So just a day after she arrived, I gave her this snuff that the termites make out of wood that breaks down all the obstacles, and she went into the water to surrender to her ancestors.

She didn't get trance possessed, my Auntie, but the spirit came. "He had such grief," she said, and she wept. And I wept too. The violence that the Jews have suffered we Africans also have suffered.

We went to Botswana the next day. Deena's spirits called her to Mandlovu, the elephant. We came to the white bones of an elephant along the road. I saw clearly how her father sat in her now because she left an orange in the bones as an offering and said to the elephant, "They tried to kill my people too. We are peacemakers. We have come to meet you." And the elephants came to meet us that day. That's the way these peacemaking spirits operate—my Auntie's father bringing together the elephants and the people.

26
HEALING BY NUMBERS

Crossing the threshold back to the hospital from the woods was nothing if not dramatic. I was a little frightened, of course, but also bright eyed and bushy tailed with the idealism of a healer who is still impossibly young, a nurse who has, with some humor, taken on the role of resident *nganga* at the UCLA Medical Center.

I was sent to a neurology floor where I was given five patients, one of whom was a severely mentally retarded man in his late twenties. "Failure to thrive" was the diagnosis, which is to say he decided to stop eating. His mother didn't know what to do, so she had him hospitalized. We put a nasogastric tube down his nose and into his stomach to pump food into him and strapped his wrists to the bed so he wouldn't pull it out. He had pulled it out already once the first day, and shortly after I arrived, hands or no hands, he managed to do so again. I had to stick another tube in. What else to do? Let him starve?

I do not like sticking things down people's noses, not the suction catheters that draw secretions from people's lungs, not the trumpets we jam in and tape to the patient so the suction catheters don't overtraumatize the cartilage of the nose, and certainly not nasogastric tubes which, when a patient resists, are nearly impossible to advance to the stomach. Needless to say, this fellow resisted with everything he had in him.

For the tube to go into the stomach and not the lungs, the head must be tilted completely forward, chin to chest. I tried to convince this mentally retarded man that the torture I was about to visit upon him was for his own good. I gently and firmly pressed on the back of his head as I pushed the tube in. He responded by arching his neck back while he sputtered and screamed out and spit on me. I asked for assistance from a couple of other nurses, and after advancing the tube for virtually a foot into his body, I was sure that I was successful, that we could continue feeding him.

I was wrong. I placed the end of the tube that was not in his body in a cup of water. Bubbles indicated that it was lodged deep in his lungs. I was afraid that perhaps I had injured him. I'd never seen a catheter extend so far down the bronchial tree. When I withdrew the tube, I was relieved to see that there was no blood at the end of it.

The man looked at me with stark terror, unanswerable and uncomprehending. I placed my hand quietly on his shoulder and sang an African song to the father of light, not knowing for sure whether extending tenderness to someone you have tortured intensifies the torture or softens it. I was grateful to be transferred to another floor before I was obligated to try inserting a nasogastric tube a second time.

I rely on my patients to remind me I am a *nganga* when I am lost in the ordinary violence of the work that I do. Another floor, another world, another little nest of possibilities. My savior that night was an old Jewish man who had just found out his cancer had spread from lungs to brain. He was what we call a "sundowner;" pleasant and lucid in the day but through the night quite out of his mind.

After midnight I walked into his room, and he was straining against his wrist restraints and crying out. Over and over he said, "It is a terrible thing to die on Yom Kippur." I glanced at his wrist and at the crude tatoo: *kazetzik*, a concentration camp survivor. I remembered a cold afternoon I spent at Auschwitz-Birkenau with Deena, squatting in the mud in the shambles of the old crematorium and planting a few kernels of blue corn. I was surprised that the Polish mud was still thick with splinters of bone almost fifty years later.

"I know where you are," I told him. "It is a dreadful place. I can't make this better than it is, but I can pray with you." I held his hand, and together we chanted the Hebrew *Shema*, "Here O Israel, the Lord our God is One." In the morning he told me of the terrible dream he had in which we prayed together and then laughed apologetically for wasting my time with such a dream.

I've heard it said that the kindest of the Buddhas live in Hell. I knew this to be true because I once lived in the hell realms and know the kindness that was extended to me. Suffering calls forth Buddha's mind to meet it: bright, skillful, and generous.

Everything seems to be a matter of crossing thresholds—invisible boundaries that separate worlds—entering the woods or leaving them; the parting of the electric doors of the hospital as I enter or leave into the cold morning air; passing that threshold as one approaches the bed of unimaginable suffering; leaving the bedside to the comradery of peers. And of course there is that threshold between Africa and America. I hope to bring a little of the intelligence that I was initiated into back to a world that contradicts it on every level, but where I insist that it thrive against whatever odds—thrive and be honored.

The last time I was in Zimbabwe, the Zimbabwean dollar was worth half of what it had been a few months before. The price of maize went up, and poor people were rioting in the street. As my plane left Johannesburg, CNN was broadcasting the news of the moment—something to do with the adventures of Bill Clinton's sex life. My heart sank. I was aware that I was returning to a country that was on the verge of psychosis and terminal narcissism.

My friendship with you, *mapatya*, has delivered me to the far edge of an imperial domain. Here is an economic and cultural imperialism, brutal and predictable in its greed but part of it is also Western medicine, no less an Imperium—no less greedy, no less hungry for territory, no less infatuated with its certainties, no less disdainful of other ways of knowing.

When you complain of the *ngangas* who think they can heal without listening to their ancestors and then kill so many people with herbs, I think of the recent study that found that the fourth most common cause of death in American hospitals are prescribed medications. These are properly prescribed medications, mind you, given under direct and constant medical supervision. There is no way to estimate the number killed by medications away from institutions, but one could easily guess it to be in the hundreds of thousands every year. In light of this, the American debate over doctor-assisted suicide seems quaint: to undergo medical care itself is to take your life into your own hands despite the Hippocratic Oath that all doctors swear to, "First, do no harm."

We rely so much on the magic of numbers, and by numbers we attempt to heal people: a medical regimen based on statistics and lab values manipulated with drugs and blood products while the person of the patient is often nearly ignored. Or a culture of "time management" that has doctors and nurses flitting from patient to patient as if performing purely mechanical tasks along an assembly line. And this is driven by the dollars and cents that the insurance company will pay or refuse to pay for this treatment or that. Numbers, numbers, numbers.

In this flurry of numbers, the West has set itself separate and above the most basic tenets of hundreds of thousands of years of healing tradition on this planet—which is to say it has placed itself beyond the reach of the ancestors. We split things down and then split them again and again. Body split from mind, self from community, community from the natural world and all of it split from the felt presence of Spirit.

I write these bitter words at the hospital itself, in a cancer ward, at 3:00 a.m. I have a brief break as my patients sleep. Already I distrust the bitterness; too simple, too much certainty, and thus untrustworthy. Yes, one must rage against the organized lovelessness of any institution, but there are other stories. I confess that part of my commitment to the hospital is that it confounds me, regularly undoes me, shows me the superficiality of my thinking and my loving.

Last week, for example, I came to care for a man the last few days of his life and care for his family also. He was thirty-seven years old, at the end stage AIDS with a rare form of cancer that had eaten away much of his face. He frightened people, of course, but for reasons I can't understand. I saw only beauty in him. On my breaks he would sleep, and I'd meditate and pray at his bedside.

Though it was clear he had little time to live, doctor after doctor continued writing orders of aggressive treatment that, I felt, did not honor the moment but seemed to prolong an agonizing death. His whole body was giving out—what we call "multisystems failure." He was confused and had fallen out of bed twice. And so we strapped him in his bed. He screamed, "Untie me, I am not an animal," until we had to sedate him.

I was charting my nurse's notes when a young doctor looked up my patient's lab values on the computer and decided that he needed blood. Numbers! "Why?" I asked. "His kidneys are shutting down. His body is trying to die. What he needs now is to be made comfortable. A little love at his bedside."

She heard me and scratched out the order. "I don't know how you do this work," she said. "I have four patients like him, and I don't know what to do. It is so sad. How do you return to this every night?"

The following night I walked into his room and found him lying in blood, pooled around his mouth and eyes, gurgling. I called a nurse's aide to my side, and we elevated him and tried to stop the bleeding from his nose and mouth. We used pressure dressing, ice, and a dab of lidocaine that I hoped would freeze the veins. But no luck. We couldn't stop him from bleeding.

I went to the computer and looked up his lab values. As I suspected, the part of his blood that makes it clot was depleted. Suddenly it was me who was arguing for blood. Nobody should die of bleeding from the face. I felt sympathy then for the young doctor who kept faith with numbers, and although she couldn't bear to look at this man, I knew that she was struggling with the impossible, with how small we all are before the reality of suffering.

27

THEY ARE RAINMAKERS

If you ask me about healing, I have to talk about the water spirits because they are the ones that heal. I do not. I am their servant.

We call the water spirits because other spirits tell us that these water spirits are the most powerful of all the spirits. They say they communicate directly with God. They are just like his angels. They do not pray to any other spirits in between them. They have tremendous power of healing and wisdom direct from the Creator. They are water, they are air, they are clouds, they are rainmakers. This is what I understand about water spirits. These are the spirits that make use of me. It is these spirits who started telling me that they were the healers, and they laid down steps that I should follow in my healing.

The first step is that I should tell that person, however sick he or she is, that they should go and talk to their spirits so that we can be guided and led by them. Their spirits will talk to them through dreams. My spirits have given me the power to understand the language of dreams so when people come to me with their dreams, I can tell what their spirits want me to do for this or that person. Then I pray over water so that it has power, and I take him into the water.

My spirits then say, "You take that herb, that herb, that herb, that herb, which is going to heal that person who has got, say, skin diseases, eye diseases, headaches, stomach pains, and so forth. Let him go under that water where you have put those herbs.

He goes in the water. I'm just standing by. He goes under several times, turning over. Then my spirits will tell me, "That's all. That's enough now," and I tell him to come out of the water.

"Let's do some light exercises," I say. Or my spirits say, "Take this patient into the sweat lodge with some smoke and light herbs," like we did yesterday here. When we do that, many evil spirits are chased away.

"Take some herbs to eat. If you have any stomach pains, chest pains, what-what, they will disappear with my herbs."

Then I give them some more herbs to put in their porridge to work on their blood circulation, respiratory system. For everything they take herbs.

I usually work with a person for three days. After three days I will tell him, "You go and see your doctor." When they come back to me, I want to hear the report from the doctor.

The problem is with people who come from very far. They need accommodations, and our house is so little. And they need food to eat as well. You know it. So many of these people who come from far away— some come from Zambia, some come from South Africa. Some come from Malawi or Mozambique. They come here saying, "There is no-where else to go!" So I've got to take care of them. We manage.

The way I operate is I don't look at one disease in a person. There are multiple diseases in a person, so many of them in one individual person. That disease you may see which may be detected by the machines may exclude other diseases which are in a person. I cure a variety of diseases because I use so many different types of herbs. This water mermaid, Ambuya Chop-chop, shows me flowers, and this Old Man shows me other herbs. I mix them together and feed them to my patients in por-ridge.

An original treatment, yes. Ah hah! An original treatment, then we go into other things. Usually my spirits tell me what else to do, and that person's spirits as well will give him dreams on what else to do. So I work with their dreams and my dreams as well. That way the spirits are in agreement.

Sometimes a person comes here who has been having dreams for years. Then all of a sudden the dreams stop coming. I know there is some work to be done there.

There is a communication breakdown between him and his spirits. I call upon my spirits to tell me what to do to bring back the dreams, and I give him an herb which is a snuff like *bute*. I give him just a bit, and the thing that has been blocking him from talking to his spirits will disap-pear. Tomorrow he will say to me, "I've had now this dream."

The healing that I do comes naturally. You are born with these spirits and then initiated so they can make use of you. You see all the herbs I have here? Every one of them I saw in my dreams and then went to the bush to gather them.

People come to me to cast out *ngozi*. In English I call *ngozi* "evil spirits," but that's only because there is no word for *ngozi* in your language. They are not evil, but they can be destructive. What they want is justice.

For example there was a great healer who married away from her village into a new family. She used herbs to heal the people and made a lot of money in her husband's home. In our tradition, when you marry someone who is a healer, you take part of the wages from the healing to her relatives so that the two families remain united and the spirit that is upon the healer is at peace. Unfortunately in this family they didn't do that. They used all of the riches from this spirit and shared nothing with the spirit's living family.

When this woman died, she left behind herds of cattle, goats, money, and other property. Her husband's family didn't want to share any of it. So the dead woman became an *ngozi* in the village, and many years later trance possessed one of her own granddaughters, who became sick, mentally disturbed.

This granddaughter came across a man who told her about me, and when she came to me, I saw the problem and talked to her about it. She fully understood.

So what I did was I took her to Victoria Falls and performed a powerful ritual. I invited this dead woman to trance possess this young woman because I wanted to talk to the *ngozi* face to face.

The *ngozi* came, and I said, "Look at this. This woman you are trance possessing and torturing did not commit any offense. She did not do anything at all. What I want is for you to free this woman because I'm going to send her to your village to talk with your people. Then something can be done to make peace."

This *ngozi* wept and said, "You are helping me now." Wept. Then the *ngozi* said, "I will guide this young woman to my people because I can see that her brother is willing to help make peace between these two families. I free her from this moment."

When the spirit left her, I told this young woman what had expired, and she went to her brother that same day. He was willing to do what the *ngozi* said. He and his mother went to the relative of the *ngozi*, and they agreed that they should settle this thing out immediately. It was done, and the relatives of the deceased brewed beer to welcome back their spirit. Right up to now, this woman is a free woman. That is how problems with *ngozi* can be settled.

28
CIRCLES WITHIN CIRCLES WITHIN CIRCLES

It wasn't always this way. Western humoral medicine, as venerable a tradition as the elemental medicine of China and India, saw that the body is made up of earth, fire, water, and air. At the beginning of the seventeenth century, no doctor would be trusted if he didn't have a grasp of medical astrology. Western medicine had not yet been reduced to technical intervention in a machine-like body. A whole cosmos stood behind and within the act of healing. Like Bantu medicine the body existed within circles of relationship. It has been a great gift, Augustine, that you have returned me to a medical way of knowing that perceives the circles within the circles within the circles: self, family, clan, and tribe encircled by the ancestors; the ancestors encircled by the elemental intelligences of earth, fire, water, and air. All of it encircled by the endless presence of God. It seems to me that Bantu medicine is about reconciliation within a field of relationships.

The first time I looked over the edge of the medical Imperium and saw a profound way of medical knowing that was not Western was when Deena and I were taking care of Hella when she was dying of liver cancer. A couple of weeks before Hella died, Deena asked her if there was anything about the cancer which she had never expressed.

"Well," said Hella, "there were the porcupines. When I was a young woman, I was living with my kids in upstate New York, and our cabin was infested with porcupines. I beat one to death with a shovel. We didn't know any better back then. A day hasn't gone by since then when I haven't thought about it. Sometimes the cancer feels like that porcupine poking me with its quills inside my body."

When Hella told Deena this story, I was reading quite a lot about Navajo healing. Among the Navajo such a story would be taken seriously because disease originates when the patterns of beauty—*hozro*—are ruptured in acts such as Hella's. Had Hella been Navajo, she would have gone to a hand trembler or crystal gazer for diagnosis and told what singing ceremony might be effective in reweaving her back into the way of beauty, which is to say back into health.

Shortly after Hella died, Deena and I were in New Mexico, and I had the opportunity to tell her story to a Navajo man. He told me that a rash had broken out over his arms and shoulders so he went to a hand trembler for diagnosis.

Going into a trance, that diagnostician scratched a design in the sand with his shaking hand and, reading it, said, "You have offended the red ant people." He confessed that he had poured kerosene on an ant mound by his house and lit them on fire.

Hella's story and the story of this Navajo fellow cast an incident in my own life in a new light. When I was eleven years old and my parents divorced, I took out my rage on the local insects, especially the ants. I upturned anthills with a shovel or blew them up with firecrackers, and yes, I enjoyed the image of chaos—dousing a nest with gasoline and lighting it afire.

For three years I had terrible eczema in my inner arms, flaking, bleeding. The Western diagnosis might be psychosomatic. Some estimate that eighty percent of skin problems have a psychological origin. Had I gone to a homeopathic doctor, she might celebrate. In homeopathy skin problems indicate that a disease has migrated outward from one's core and is being sloughed off. In homeopathy it's actually ill advised to treat such a condition because you risk driving it back in and, in the long run, precipitating a serious disease.

Had I gone to a hand trembler, he likely would have understood that I'd violated the *wolachi'i dine'e* and that I needed a Red Antway ceremony. Instead I was taken to a dermatologist who simply prescribed cortisone cream which dealt with the symptom effectively but had no effect whatsoever on the disease. Eventually it disappeared on its own as eczema often does as my rage quieted down a bit.

These are three different ways of medicine. Homeopathy stands at the edge of the Imperium, but Navajo, like Bantu medicine, is far beyond the edge as are all the medical traditions of colonialized people. To believe that the natural world is inspirited, as Native American and African people do, and to know that there are consequences to the violence we do to that spiritual domain—at best such beliefs are exoticized or sentimentalized, at worst dismissed as superstitious and backward. Rarely are they honored as real medicine moving on a logic entirely different than the medicine of the Imperium.

We have talked of these things so many times, and if I'm honest, you and I know, *mapatya*, that the corruption and disintegration of Bantu medicine is really no different in its own way from that in Western medicine. Nonetheless, I have a fond memory of sitting with you in Bulawayo and of all things, "E.R." came onto the television.

"So that's what you do for a living, is it?" you said.

"Oh, yes," I responded, a little embarrassed at how swept up I was by the melodrama, and more than a little humored at the nostalgia I felt for the hospital as I sat in the house of shaman. There is dignity to the work I do, I thought. In spite of everything I will insist that the hospital be a place where I practice the way of the ancestors.

29
I DID NOT APPLY TO BE A *NGANGA*

In the police force I was doing tremendous work that the police recognized entirely. Most of the policemen would come to me for help if they were being tormented by *ngozi* or worried by their ancestors. During that time it was unusual for a *nganga* to operate from the police camp, but with me it was smooth sailing at first.

Trouble started when people who were not members of the police force wanted my assistance. They were coming from the surrounding townships. They came in hundreds each day. The main gate was manned by a police official. Not everyone was allowed in the camp. So there was trouble at the main gate.

"Where do you want to go?"

"To Augustine."

The next one, "To Augustine."

The whole day, people "to Augustine." And through the weekend as well. All of this was written down in a book: your address, where you come from, where you are going, who you wanted to see.

The whole book was almost full of Augustine, Augustine. Then the senior police official said, "This is a problem now. What are you going to do?"

I said, "I don't know."

He said, "You are a *nganga*?"

I said, "Oh, yes. I am." I was also a chief inspector, by then a high rank in the police force in Zimbabwe.

He said, "Why can't we do it this way? You work with members of the police force only and leave out the rest of the people."

"If this is what you want me to do, you put a signpost at the gate there—you, not me. Tell the public that they are not allowed to be healed by Augustine."

They gave orders to the young boy who manned the gate, "Whoever is not a policeman is not allowed in."

There was a big gathering outside of people who had come to see me one by one. They said, "If this is the case, we are going to report this to the *Chronicle*, to the newspaper. Augustine does not belong to the policemen. He is for everybody." In that group were Ndebele people, Shona people, and other tribes. "This is what we are going to do. We are going to demonstrate." So they laid face down.

At first the police said, "For now let him operate." But soon the senior police official said, "Either you find a house somewhere else or stop operating as a *nganga*."

I said, "It is impossible for me to stop operating as a *nganga*. I did not apply to be a *nganga* at all." He also laughed the way you are laughing because he knew what I meant.

I got a house in one of the townships with a small room. So it wouldn't do. Then I came to this place at 33 Investon Road. The woman who owned the house was also one of my patients. She said, "I think I've got better premises for you to operate from." I worked from that house for quite some time.

While all this was going on, I was told I was to be transferred from Bulawayo back to Harare. It was quite a promotion. I was to have more salary and more allowances because I would be traveling from province to province. I was to be in charge of all the police schools in the country.

A man came from Harare to take over my job. He came to look at the new stations. I showed him everything for a week. He was to begin the takeover the following Monday, but on Sunday I had a dream. My spirits came and said, "Tomorrow, Monday morning at eight o'clock, you go and get complete resignation forms. You are no longer going to be a policeman. We want you to do our work only. Go and do that Monday morning." The dream came three times. And I saw in that dream myself going to the first office with my resignation forms and saying, "Please sign here. I am leaving."

I did exactly this. Two days later they called me and said, "How on earth are you going to tell us that you are resigning!"

I said, "That's final, sir. Please put your signature here."

They phoned Harare, they phoned here and there. I said, "Please, I want your signature. I'm leaving."

They did it. So I left the police force. I should be in Harare right now. Right now! But the spirits wanted me among Ndebele people. This is my work. This is my home.

30
GRANDMOTHER SPIDER

You have always told me that human beings can't heal, that only God and the spirits can heal. "The spirits are God's legs and arms," you say, "and we are also God's legs and arms." Who are the spirits that make use of me in the hospital? How has the hospital become the sacred domain where I serve spirit?

Without Ambuya Buwebuwe, Grandmother Spider, I could never practice as a healer in the hospital. I am utterly reliant on her complexity, agility, her many minds, and the subtlety with which she can fold even the most excruciating moments into exquisite beauty.

People who think that humans carry the best of nature's intelligence have never watched a spider slide across a web, eight legs perfect in their coordination and placement. Embodied brilliance at its most graceful, this one spins the web of interconnection from her own body and never gets entangled in it. And at the end of a night of hunting when the web is ragged and torn, she swallows it and recycles it through her gut to spin it out again when night falls. For seven years I've looked in every nook and cranny for a living spider to sing to in the hospital without success. She is, nevertheless, present.

My favorite Spider Woman story comes from the Hopi Indians. They say that one winter solstice, it seemed as if the sun had drifted so far out of orbit it might never come back, and all beings would be left behind in the dark and perish. The animals came together in council. Bear roped the sun, but for all his strength couldn't pull it forward a single inch. Wolf tried but was no more successful than Bear. Finally Spider Woman with her small voice said, "I can do it," and everyone laughed at the idea of the old woman even trying. The Ambuya cast a thread through her spinnerets and with little effort at all drew the sun back in.

This story has a truth which is that the delicate gesture of casting out the thread of interconnection succeeds where brute strength and will power fails. In the hospital this casting out the thread is largely what I do as a healer. Because I move night after night to different floors in a ten-story hospital, Ambuya Buwebuwe has been able to spin a stunning and complex web that has transformed my workplace into a village.

A *nganga* apparently requires a village, or he is just a cipher among spirits. My cards open doors, and for many I have become the one who reads the oracle, the dream teller, the one who looks at things from the angle of the mysteries. Sometimes, because I rarely work with the same people two nights in a row, I feel like something of a gypsy. Often I'm embarrassed when someone whose face I scarcely recognize brings up a card reading I had done months or years previous, vividly remembering it and presuming I do also. Sometimes it's clear that they had bared their souls to me or that I had shifted their lives in some small way. But when I am the oracle, my words are not my words. The spider knows that beauty is in the making of beauty, in the very act of it, in the care with which she spins the web.

As with you, Augustine, the sick and the dying, that community within a community, come and go and call out for kindness. Again, it is the spider that comes forth to draw them back into orbit or to draw the *nganga*'s spirit to the bedside. She is so poised in her alertness, this grandmother, always looking for the way of connection, the way of making beauty.

I had a patient a couple of years ago who had cancer of the jaw, so they removed it. An attempt was made at reconstructing his face with tissue from his thigh, the result being that it looked like raw meat, swollen and oozing with a hole for a mouth. He could neither eat nor talk and breathed mostly through a tracheotomy in his neck that was always spewing sputum. I had seen him a couple of days before I was assigned to be his nurse, and his face both repulsed and frightened me. It is rare that I feel this kind of visceral reaction to a patient, however grotesque, but my eyes smarted to look at the man. I could barely stand to be in his presence, and because I had a patient who shared a room with him, I found myself quickly skirting past his bed and its half-closed curtains as if I were endangered by some sort of monster. So when I was assigned to be this man's nurse, I swallowed and smiled to myself; the reckoning. I attended first to all my other patients so that when I approached this man's bed, I would be unhurried and alert to the thread that would connect him and me. Unhurried alertness is what invites the grandmother in. When I hurry, she flees.

The thread was immediately obvious—small talk with his wife and changing his gown with her, which was soaked in sputum. Observing her undisguised loving and the mixture of pain, gratitude, and humor in his eyes. I said, "I'm moved to watch the sweetness between the two of you. I have a sharp eye for a good marriage because I am blessed with one. I see that you are too."

"We celebrated our fiftieth last week," she said.

"Fifty years together!" I said, trying to imagine it. "My wife and I have been together for merely ten."

I looked at her husband, and he was weeping. If he had a mouth, I think he would also be smiling, but his eyes were expressive enough. For the life of me, I could no longer see a monster. I saw a man who was luminous in the presence of love.

I emphasize order and beauty because those are Spider Woman's mysteries; beauty and order woven together at a deep and organic level, at the level of the heart.

31
SIMAKUHLE AND GEORGE

Simakuhle had some dreams that she was going to be my wife. She was my patient. She wanted some help. I was married then, and one important thing that my spirits told me from the beginning was that I should never, ever go about with any other women. But she was given such direct dreams, and when she used to tell me them with other people sitting around, I wondered where these dreams were leading. They were precisely saying that Simakuhle was not to marry anyone of her tribe. Simakuhle was never to get married to anybody except Augustine. She didn't know my first name. I didn't even know her first name. I had nothing to do with her in relation to love, nothing totally. I was strict with my spirits, very strict. Whatever they say, I accepted that, and they said, "You mustn't go along with any other woman except the wife that you are married to."

So I'd listened to her dreams. I could feel my heart beat. I was scared of these dreams. It was like this for two, three, four, five years. Then she was told that she should prepare some *sadza* and feed me. I said, "How can that be done? She's not my wife at all."

Trouble started with my wife. Each time I went to bed, I would be trance possessed while I was asleep. She could not understand. She thought I was ill. She told the relatives about this issue, her parents, who were still living. They said, "Your husband has ancestral spirits which are working on him."

She didn't like it. She was a Christian. It went on like that. Finally it came out in the open, and she said, "You are very sick."

I said, "Yes, I am a sick man."

She said, "I don't believe these are good spirits on you."

I was silent to that.

She said, "I cannot be with a man with such spirits. I'm going to divorce you."

I said, "Okay." I never argued with her.

So we went to the courts, and the magistrate asked, "Do you have something to say?"

I said, "Yes. I love my wife. It is unfortunate because I am a sick man. She cannot stay with a sick man at all. My illness is about the spirits."

The magistrate said, "We are not giving you a period of separation because I, the magistrate, understand about ancestral spirits. I am giving you an immediate divorce."

She said, "What I want from this man is the house in Harare. It must be mine."

I said, "Okay. What else?"

She said, "I want everything in this house."

I said, "Okay. What else?"

She said, "Our four children. They are all mine."

I said, "Okay. What else?"

She said, "I want you to transport all these things I have here in Bulawayo for me to my house in Harare."

This I did. I approached a moving company, and they moved everything. Everything including some of my clothes. And when it was done, I said, "Have you taken everything that you want?"

She said, "I want maintenance for these children."

I said, "How much do you want?"

She went to court and said, "I want your pension."

I said, "Fine. Please look after my children. Goodbye."

Simakuhle's dreams became more powerful. They were saying, "This woman was not for you at all. Look at her heart. We are giving you a wife. She is a sick woman. She is a poor woman. This is your wife for life." That is how we came to be.

She was sick, Simakuhle. Remember I told you that she was going to go to the hospital and have a heart operation, so I took her. We comforted one another. She supports the work that I do very much, and I support her spiritually. That is how I got Simakuhle into my house, and that is how I found myself in Simakuhle's home as well.

The spirits have given me Simakuhle not only as my wife but also as my sister. Instructions about how I should work in this community are given to Simakuhle by my spirits and by her spirits. She has the gift of receiving messages through her dreams so that in the morning she tells me what I should do. Because my spirits talk to me while I'm doing the work, they know I need to sleep at night. They would rather give Simakuhle all the dreams so I can rest.

This unites the two of us. No one can do a perfect job alone. One needs some help from other people. My help comes from Simakuhle. When I'm initiating people, Simakuhle has dreams about the whole group. This is helpful, very helpful, indeed. Remember in the *Torah* prophets were sent with messages for people. We must have prophets among us to do this work properly. Dreamers like my wife are priceless.

For example Simakuhle will say to me, "This morning there is going to come a man with powerful evil spirits, and when you work with him, you must put on a leopard-skin belt and use the buffalo tail to chase that spirit away." She'll even tell me what kind of herbs to use. She will tell me these things first thing in the morning, and twenty minutes later the man appears. I just follow what was given to her in her dream, and the work is done.

Often I will go to a village to do ritual work, and when I come back, I will be told by Simakuhle that I must smoke this herb or that herb because I was handling some difficult spirits. And then she tells me to go into the water.

I can be a powerful dreamer myself. I can dream about what is going to happen to the whole world, to the president of such and such a country, or I'll be told they want me to rest because the work I do requires a lot of physical power, of thinking, and meditating. Before I got married to Simakuhle, I was a dreamer, but now things are rather changed because there is too much work on me. As I look back on these years of marriage, I can see that her ancestors and mine were married before we were even born at all, and they wanted to maintain that link.

My firstborn, George, also stands alongside me. When he looks at me, he can tell when I'm not happy. He sees it deeply. I can see his face shrinking. At times I can see the tears running down his cheeks. He is getting that something is going on inside of me because I don't want to tell him how much I suffer for the family. I know I would be giving him too much of a burden to carry. He is young, so I don't like to be open to him. But what he senses in me is my love for my children. He sees that. He sees how much I suffer for the family.

32
FINAL RITES

Although many cultures, including the Bantu, see disease as something that sometimes opens the path to initiation, there are few surviving cultures that have initiatory ordeals equal in severity to what happens routinely in a modern hospital. In traditional cultures such ordeals have always been about moving into a more profound and inclusive order. Miraculously some patients actually find a path through the wilderness of their affliction into a deeper understanding of their place in the universe and are therefore healed.

One of my patients was a man named Jim. Jim was in his early forties and had a rather large brain tumor. By the time I met him, he had gone through a full ordeal—months of chemotherapy and the regimen of sleeplessness that hospitals prescribe to every patient. His prognosis was poor, and he knew it. He had appreciated my skills as a nurse and decided to avail himself to my skills as a *nganga*. We scheduled a date for a healing ceremony.

The ritual was simple enough, and Jim's stay in the hospital had been so merciless that he was well prepared to go deep. Between the cancer and the almost hallucinatory psychological effects of the steroids he was taking to bring down the swelling in his brain, one might say he was vulnerable to the movement of spirit. Although in truth he probably had only a few months to live, we acted as if he had only a couple of hours left. Outside on our land, under the night sky, I left him alone to make closure on his life, ask forgiveness and forgive, if that made sense, and reach for the deepest meanings of what it had all been about. I encouraged him towards the prayer of gratitude because to die without gratitude makes for a miserable passage.

When I returned, we talked, and then I invoked the spirits with songs and offerings and took him in his imagination to the threshold of the village of the ancestors. By smashing a coconut, I ritualized the moment of his death. Leaving him sleeping under the moon, I had no doubt that he was among the ancestors and that his dream would be a profound one.

Some say the village of the ancestors is under the sea or deep in the forest, *mapatya*. I remember you visited it at the bottom of the Zambezi. In Jim's dream he was digging and digging with vigor until he came upon an ancient Jewish library filled with old and venerable books. When he awoke, I entered into the dream with him, delighting in the awe and pleasure he felt when he reached the underground library.

After immersing him in water and taking him through a ritual of rebirth, he headed home. He spent the final few months of his life with me and the kaballist Rabbi Jonathan Omer-Man as his allies, setting up camp in the sanctuary of the Word.

One afternoon his wife Anne invited me to their house. It was to be my great honor to do the final rites. Jim was ebullient, tranquil, and ready. Our conversation was often interrupted by his need to confer with invisible presences. Anne had become quite familiar with these presences —by then they were family. These presences seem to gather at the bedside of people who are about to cross over.

The ritual was the same as before, this time excluding the rites of rebirth. The shattered coconut I placed at the four corners of the bed. The following day Jim sank into a coma, emerging for a moment to kiss his little boy goodnight. A few hours later, he was dead.

Spider Woman is in love with the configuration and reconfiguration of meaning. In Jim's case meaning was not annihilated by death; death brought it to fulfillment. Beyond that, Jim's death was itself an act of healing—no one who was in touch with him during the end of his life was left unchanged. In the village of the ancestors, he clearly learned that dying can be a fine art. His death was, among other things, a well crafted gift to the community.

Configurations and reconfigurations, Augustine, they are everywhere, and they are always changing. As a *nganga* I am always entering into them: the presence of this particular patient or family, this specific way of making meaning, this way of healing. I think of cat's cradle, one of Spider Woman's gifts to the Navajo—reality remade this way and that. A certain dexterity seems to be required in intelligence, imagination, and compassion.

Earlier I was talking about how my eczema might be seen from a Navajo or homeopathic angle, and how it was treated by a dermatologist. My disease was the Grandmother speaking. She is lucid in placing different ways of medical knowing side by side and appreciating what they can see and cannot see. Having labored in the salt mines of Western medicine for twenty years, my persistent prayer is that someday it will be able to see beyond itself.

33
AND THEN THE RAIN FELL

The spirits said in a dream, "So many people are going to initiate you. The Zulu, the Shona, the Ndebele, the Karanga, even white people will initiate you."

One day I was in the Matopo Hills in a cave, and I dreamt I saw a young white boy running in front of me and then disappearing. I said, "Where is my brother? Have you seen my brother? I'm looking for my brother here."

People in that cave said, "He went this way." I looked for this brother, but I couldn't find him. Two or three months later, Michael appeared.

Michael, my twin brother, appeared after having that dream where I was looking for my young brother who was in the cave at Matopo. I thought that I was actually going to initiate Michael, which was correct. And I thought it would just end there.

After initiating Michael and taking him to secret places where he was asked by his spirits to go, it was my chance to be initiated by him. I didn't ask Michael to initiate me, but the spirits had a conversation about this one. They talked. The issue was going to be solved by him initiating me in a deep way, a deep, more advanced basis.

After praying so hard together, we went to Victoria Falls, called by Africans, *Moziyatunya*, the smoke that thunders. On the way, fortunately, we had a cassette tape from Deena. It was powerful for me because it described what was going to happen on our way to Victoria Falls step-by-step. It was a time of drought, but she said we were going to meet the spirits in the form of rain, and just as she said it, they appeared. We came out of the car and stood under the showers. She said we were going to meet the spirits in the form of wild animals, and they appeared. Elephants crossed the road, and we stopped and went to meet them. In that tape she was describing it as though she was there physically. Before we came to the river, I said to Michael, "I feel like someday I'm going to meet Deena. There is a call."

At the river he gave offerings to the wild animals and taught me how to do it. He gave some offerings to the spirits of the water. He laid me down, said his prayers, and prepared me to enter the spiritual world. Talking to me gently all the time, he prayed for me and sang for me, and for the first time in my life outside of my dreams, my spirits came through —I was trance possessed.

They all came through me, one after another. In my trance possession I saw visions. My spirits showed me their village under the river—a big village, green and blue with ancestors from every race. From this village Spider Woman, *Ambuya Buwebuwe*, came to me for the first time. The black eagle who protects the innocent came, and so did the white eagle, the peacemaker. These spirits and others took over my body and took Michael in their arms to initiate him. They wanted to show him their power and wisdom because they were happy, because they were now free.

Before the spirits left, they actually asked Michael to go in the water. There Michael was totally taken over by Spider Woman. The powers that were put into his body were tremendous.

When my spirits left me, I wept. I wept bitterly in Michael's arms and for a long time because I couldn't believe that Michael could have done such work. I couldn't believe that it was him who had done this work at all. It was unbelievable. But there is a white man—this is what I thought—who is my brother and who is liberating my spirits. It was unbelievable. He had done it.

When his spirits left him, he also wept in my arms. In the end we both wept. I was in his arms, he was in my arms, and we wept. Then the rain fell, a downpour. I think it rained all night.

One cannot liberate one's own spirits; somebody must come and liberate your spirits for you. That is why my spirits called *mapatya* to Africa. My spirits were wounded spirits, and they needed somebody to do an initiation to heal the wound. Otherwise they would remain suffering. Spirits are from one source. They did not care that *mapatya* was white. They do not look at the color of skin.

So that is my initiation by Michael, in short. It has made it possible for me to come into the hands of my spirits directly.

This is very interesting because I never in the first place thought that I could be trance possessed. I operated as a *nganga* for many years without being trance possessed. I was just working with people's dreams and with the herbs and nothing else. I never got trance possessed in my lifetime until after this initiation. That is how things started to change.

My trance possession at this stage is different, really, from how other people get trance possessed because my spirits can trance possess me powerfully, and yet I still know exactly what I'm doing though I cannot control myself. I cannot control my speech, I cannot control my movements, but I still know what is taking place. Other people don't remember anything at all when they are trance possessed. You have to tell them over and over again what was said by the spirits which have trance possessed them. But this is not the case with me, no. I know everything.

Augustine is actually removed from me. I don't see him. It's rather that he is hidden somewhere. Then the spirits come in and take over. Each time the spirits come and trance possess me, I feel that I'm going. I am being overpowered by these spirits. And I can tell that if this kind of a spirit is coming, it wants that and that and that, and I will prepare for its coming. It's difficult to know how I can tell what spirit is coming. It's difficult because with some spirits, I know by the way my heart beats. This tells me that it's a powerful spirit that is going to come. So I ask, "What do I do?"

It says, "Sit still," and it comes. At times I feel the movement of my chin, and I know the type of power that is going to come. You know, I really cannot describe the way how it is that they come.

34

NOT DELIBERATELY EATING SOULS

Simakuhle once asked me if there were many witches in America. I said, "No, not really, not people who deliberately go about eating souls, but the country is haunted by evil spirits. The hospital I work in is filled with such spirits because we do violence and pretend it is healing."

For example there was a young woman with AIDS. She had gotten it from her husband who had died already, and they had a little girl who was also HIV positive. Tragic as the situation was, this woman had the possibility of a good death if the hospital could refrain from torturing her in her helplessness. She had little pain as long as she wasn't moved. She had an order not to artificially revive her should she die. Her mother was at her bedside. Although everything indicated that she was on the edge of death, the doctor chose to prolong her dying.

One night her "numbers were off," which is to say that she had too much potassium in her blood. The doctor ordered a syrupy medication to bring the lab values into a normal range. Together we propped her up and pried her mouth open to pour the medicine in. Though she cried out in pain, she was far too lethargic to swallow, and I told the doctor that we were probably pouring the syrup directly into her lungs.

"It is so sad," said the doctor, "but we are doing everything we can for her." As it turned out, this incident was to be one of the lesser evils visited upon this woman in her final days.

The body is tortured until it has no capacity to resist, and it finally gives up the ghost—maybe. As we know, *mapatya*, such a death gives birth to *ngozi*, to avenging spirits, and the hospital is filled with them. You tell me *ngozi* cause nightmares; life-threatening nightmares. For many patients the hospital itself is such a nightmare.

35
THE WHITE EAGLE

Michael returned to Zimbabwe a few months later, and again we entered into initiating each other. I was prepared for this second initiation by a strange dream. It was back when I was still in Harare before I was initiated by this Ndebele man. I was walking past a big dam full of water when I saw a snuff container on the wayside. I said to myself, "I found myself a good snuff container. I'll come back and pick it up when I return from town." A few steps ahead, I saw another snuff container. Good luck! I now had two snuff containers. "I will come and pick them up on my way back." Then I saw a third snuff container. I said, "Ah! Here's another one." While I was saying that, there appeared from this pool of water three men.

The first man said to me, "Do you know the Peacemaker?"

I said, "No. I've only heard about him and read about him."

He said to me, "You are the Peacemaker."

The second man said the same thing, and I said also, "No, but I've heard about him."

The third man said exactly the same thing, but this time he told me in a more powerful voice, "You are the Peacemaker." I woke up, and I was very afraid.

My aunt was there. I went to tell her about this dream. She just sighed and said, "Ah! Don't talk about this dream anymore." So I kept quiet.

Several years later I went to a medium spirit because I wanted someone to initiate me. The first thing the spirit said was, "Young man, you have had a dream about seeing three snuff containers."

I said, "Yes."

He said, "Things that are coming into this world are great. It is not yet time to talk about that dream."

When Michael returned to Zimbabwe, my spirits said, "We are going to tell Michael what to do about this dream. He'll see how to go about it."

We were at these sacred pools about forty kilometers south of Bulawayo when I told Michael the dream. "I don't understand this one," I said.

He was quiet for a long time and then said, "I know what this dream means, but it frightens me."

We did some rituals together, and afterwards he said that he wanted to get a couple of beers before he tried to talk about the dream. So we drove back to Bulawayo.

On the way he asked me many hard questions. When we were in Bulawayo, we went to a bottle store and then sat in the car on a dark road talking and drinking beer.

He said, "Now I know why your spirits called me to Africa in the first place. I didn't know until now. They are talking to me, but I'm not sure if either of us are ready to call on this Peacemaker spirit. I know we both have to pray, and we have to go to Great Zimbabwe together very soon."

Right before I went to Great Zimbabwe with Michael and Simakuhle, I had another dream. I saw two white eagles coming towards me from the sky. One landed in my left arm; the other one was hovering about me. I was frightened in this dream. Then he left in my hand his feathers, and I was happy to receive those feathers. I was jumping up and down, excited, saying, "This is a precious gift."

When we went to the top of Great Zimbabwe, the white eagles appeared, not in my dreams this time but in reality. We saw them hovering above the ruins.

At Great Zimbabwe there is an old woman who is possessed by powerful water spirits. She lived under a river for seven years. The woman had a dream about us coming to see her. She told me that my hair had been plaited for the last time and I was to leave it like that. Secondly, that we must go to a bushman cave in the Matopo Hills for initiation.

As it turned out, this part of Matopo, where she directed us, I knew quite well. It was a place where my spirits had sent me to honor and make peace with the Ndebele spirits, where I left an offering of a snuff container on the grave of King Mzilikazi. And so it was that here I was taken over fully and completely by the Peacemaker.

When we went down the hill back towards Bulawayo a few hours later, I was still trance possessed. When we got down to the bottom of the hill, there appeared police officials, who wanted to know why we were there. The spirit told them to remove their shoes and to kneel down, and they did. The spirit through me told these men to look after this place, that it be clean at all times, no waste paper, no fires to be lit around this place, no one to wash in that river using soap, no cutting down of trees. "Don't disturb the nature around this place." This is what the spirit told these people. It was dark, and for a long time the Peacemaker instructed these policemen by the headlights of their car.

The spirit said, "This is my place, this is my place, this is my place." Three times he told them. Fortunately enough, the big man amongst this group of police officers here was a kraal head. He was inspector of the group here. He said tomorrow morning he was going to call for a meeting with his own people and tell them exactly what the spirit said through me.

Then the Peacemaker started telling these people one by one their problems and how to go about solving them. They all agreed that there were those problems. They even asked for the address where I lived because they wanted to come for help. This is what happened at Matopo.

In the first initiation at Big Falls, they just came and trance possessed me, but they never said anything through me. But this time they were able to talk. I am so grateful.

36
THE BLACK EAGLE

Alongside grandmother, Chapungu, the black eagle, is probably the main spirit who makes use of me in the hospital. Chapungu is so fierce in his kindness: warrior, king, peacemaker, healer par excellence. Given the nature of the terrain that a *nganga* has to walk in a hospital, I find that Chapungu is rarely far away from me.

I admit, Augustine, that when you placed the black eagle in my body during my first initiation, I scarcely believed it and couldn't imagine what it meant. Nor could I imagine who Chapungu was. But every time I am trance possessed by Chapungu, I enter further into the sharp and swift mystery of his intelligence.

We were visiting a Tanzanian trance medium and her husband, Pio, in the slums of Bulawayo along with a few Americans who we were introducing to the African spirit world. At one point we were sitting in a circle in a small room. I felt the hair stand up on the back of my neck and heard the movement of large wings, the sound of feathers parting in the wind.

I did not want to be possessed. I felt a certain shyness in front of the Americans and a desire not to be exoticized by them. I glanced over to Pio, feeling a little dizzy and sick to my stomach. "Chapungu is near," was all I said.

Pio replied, "I have something just for you." He left the room and returned with a pipe and a mottled feather from the underside of Chapungu's belly. "This is only for you," he said. "Smoke it."

After taking in the harsh smoke, even before I exhaled, I felt the wind lift my arms, the spread fingers becoming black feathers. More than anything my eyes were no longer my eyes. The sacred land of Matopo was below me, and my eyes scrutinized the landscape—whaleback expanse of red stone, a cluster of thatched houses. At the same time, I was very much in this small room, and I would plunge down, and my wings would divide each person from the spirits that were pulling them from the path: a cut of wing here and there. Chapungu's eye for the hidden niche where confusion festers was impeccable, each person's face being the same, continuous, reflective of, separate from the terrain of Matopo.

When his work was done, he departed, and I slumped over. When we walked out onto the streets, you pointed up into the sky. Chapungu was circling in the air above the neighborhood.

I do not know how to explain how it is that I could be both myself and Chapungu, both in Matopo and in this small room, or how Chapungu is very much both an eagle but also a king. Nor can I explain how it is that Chapungu's excellence in the arts of war and the arts of peacemaking are both necessary to his work as a healer. The blade he draws cuts through conflict, but he is also a formidable defender of the helpless when they are attacked by spirits. His kindness is fierce and courageous.

I was working on a cancer ward, a long shift, a full sixteen hours. Early on I'd noticed a teenage Mexican boy in the hallway outside a patient's room. He was wiry and tough looking, but he was also weeping. I was in a hurry, quite busy tending to my patients, but Chapungu noted the boy's grief the way he does—the bird's eye view of what exactly is happening in the territory he surveys.

A few hours later there was a commotion at the nurses' desk. Apparently this boy had gone into the staff bathroom, smeared liquid soap all over the floor and plugged up the sink so that the room was flooded. Security was called "to scare" the boy, I was told, "just to scare him." I found out also that the boy's mother was dying and likely wouldn't live through the night.

It would have been easy to let security deal with this problem. It was possible that the boy might, in fact, be dangerous. I doubted it, but there was no telling. Aside from that I didn't for a moment believe I had the skill to work with the situation. I had the least feel for what was going on, and I was frightened. Nonetheless Chapungu insisted that I step forward. I vaguely remembered that courage is what happens not when one is unafraid, but when one is afraid and acts anyway.

As I said earlier, unhurried alertness seems to invite Grandmother Spider; with Chapungu, it's this gesture of "stepping forward." There is a nakedness to the gesture, stark and somewhat lonely; the black eagle hovering on a current of air. As I walked to the lobby where this boy was with his large family, I thought, "Well, the worst that might happen is that I might have a scuffle." Then, "Well, perhaps I'll make a fool of myself, but it's worth the risk."

Opening the door and seeing the boy was the moment Chapungu flew in with unmediated kindness and insight, not for a moment afraid. I was most impressed with the precision of his language, not a word wasted.

The family had gathered around, embarrassed and apologetic for the trouble the boy had caused. They pressed around the boy, and I saw him fold into confusion. I addressed him in Spanish.

"I saw you in the hallway earlier, crying. When I was a little older than you, my father died, so I have some feeling for how difficult it must be to see your mother as she is. It's true that you messed up the bathroom because you have more feelings inside than you have words for. Am I right?"

"Yes," he said.

"And that you're not a bad person, and you will not cause any more trouble?"

"Yes."

"Some of the nurses were frightened, so they called security. I'll talk to the police and do what I can to send them away because I believe you are trustworthy."

Then I looked up at the family and said, "Take good care of him. His heart is breaking," at which point the boy broke down and was held by his aunt.

When I left the room, I saw security coming down the hall. They were, in effect, ready to attack. I explained to them the conversation I had with the boy and his family. Although they were reluctant to back off, I insisted and, thank God, they relented. That's Chapungu. I'm always struck by the piercing quality of his mind, without distraction, going to the heart of the situation.

The untempered blade is a source of violence. That is what I could not have understood before I was initiated by you, *mapatya*. As a young man, I did much violence not really knowing I was doing it. My sword was not only blunt, but I wielded it poorly. I was full of exuberance and bravado. Chapungu is the spirit of the tempered sword, and I am just now learning what it is to serve his wisdom.

37
THE SPIRITS COME IN
SO MANY DIFFERENT WAYS

My spirits seem to like to work with other spirits. That is why I do not know how many spirits are on me. That is why I am trance possessed now by Bushmen spirits, Zulu spirits, and so forth. They gather around me to do the work that needs to be done.

Sometimes the spirits trance possess me; sometimes they come to me in visions when I'm asleep. There are water spirits that come to me in the form of mermaids and then change form. They can even become water animals like dolphins and talk to me like that. Sometimes they come in the form of water birds like ducks and other big birds whose names I do not know. These animals and birds change into human form and talk to me. And when they leave me in my dream, they change back into water animals and just disappear. Some of them come in the form of wild animals—the elephant, the rhino. When they come to me in those forms, they advance towards me and they change into people.

Some come in the form of sky birds like Chapungu, the white eagle, the black eagle, the crow which has got black and white feathers. Some of the spirits come to me in the form of clouds. I see a thick black cloud coming down, and what do I see from the clouds? Human beings appear—Kings, the Queen. They walk towards me, and I talk to them. Then the cloud comes, it picks them up into the air, and they disappear.

Some even come in the form of stars. So bright they come. They approach me from above. They are like little angels. They come close and make a circle, and I sit in the circle. They take human form, and they talk to me.

I see people coming from the water, and they talk to me. The sun sometimes comes to me, but when the sun comes, it's so powerful. The light is so heavy. I almost cannot bear it without being trance possessed.

Even when I am awake, they come to me. Some of them come in the form of wind going around me and around me. Then it stops, and a person will appear. They will talk to me, and then they go.

They even come to me physically. I'll tell you a story about that one. One of my patients in Mutare had a dream in which he was instructed by my own spirit to take me to a mountain which is called Wedza. This is a sacred mountain in this country with a long history. This patient said that I was being called to meet my spirits at this mountain.

So we drove to Wedza—this man and other people of the community too. When we got there, we went straight to the top of the mountain where we saw some old ruins. As we sat in a circle, my patient got trance possessed by his spirits and advanced towards a small cave in the ruins. I looked inside the cave from afar and saw an object that was in coils.

The spirit of this young man started meditating and invited me to come and join him in the cave. I saw that the coils were moving slightly, and I told the spirit I was afraid to come because I sensed danger there. He insisted I should come forth. I refused.

Immediately this young man was trance possessed by one of my warrior spirits. I recognized him. He told me to come closer because the old one was waiting for me. I had no option except to move forth.

"The old man wants to put power in your body," the spirit said. "Smell."

The smell was unpleasant. Finally he said, "Put your hand underneath this thing here." This "thing" was a big snake. We call it in Shona rovambira. It's quite a dangerous and poisonous snake.

I put my hand underneath the rovambira, and it moved. Underneath there were three herbs. I was told to eat and swallow one of them. I did that. I was told to keep the other two, and the spirit would teach me how to use them at home. When I did what I was supposed to do, the snake curled up again, and we moved away from there.

That night we slept on the mountain, and in my dream I saw the cave again and also the rovambira. It was moving away from the cave, and I heard a voice say, "The old man is gone."

This is not a story. It is a true thing that happened.

38
ALL HIS DISTRESSING DISGUISES

Of all the things you have taught me about healing, Augustine, what I value most is the way you follow the patients, listen to them, stand beneath them, learn from them. I am reminded of what Mother Teresa said, that her work was to serve Christ in all his distressing disguises. I rely on my patients to continue the work of initiation when I'm not in Africa. In their anguish they call forth my spirits, and I am faced with the choice of letting the spirit move or stubbornly refusing to.

I had a patient named Jimmy. He was a wino who had nodded out in the middle of the street in a residential district of West Los Angeles. A car ran over him and left him there bleeding. When he was found the next morning, he was taken to the hospital, and a CT scan revealed the intense pressure of blood pushing between his skull and the gray matter of his brain.

A craniotomy was done and the blood siphoned off, but after surgery, he caught a staph infection in his surgical wound. It could be that Jimmy was out of his mind before his hospitalization. I don't know. But when I met him, he had been tethered to the bed, hands and feet, for a couple of weeks, urinating on himself and shouting obscenities at anyone who entered the room.

I came into his room sometime after midnight to hang an IV antibiotic only to find him covered with blood. He had somehow managed to pull out his IV line, and the open vein bled so that he was virtually soaked. I sang a quiet song to myself and sponged him off with as much tenderness as I could muster for a man who was literally spitting at me.

Afterwards I got the doctor to change the antibiotic order to a pill, but of course Jimmy refused the pill. He shouted at me that I was the

Devil and that he'd be out of his mind to take a pill from my hand.

Who could argue with the accuracy of his logic? For him hell spread out in the ten directions. To not treat him left him with a raging brain infection. To return him to the street would be dangerous to him and possibly others. In a psychiatric facility he'd be strapped down and drugged around the clock. Such a situation is humbling for someone who takes compassion seriously. Yes, for at least the duration of my shift, I was to be Jimmy's private devil.

When I returned with an IV nurse and a young Vietnamese aide, the sight of us provoked terror such as I have rarely seen. The aide sat on the bed and held down Jimmy's shoulder. I held Jimmy's hand firmly so that the IV nurse could insert the needle.

In the face of this kind of horror, it is a learned habit to place Hell in parentheses, giving it smaller dimensions as if such a drama were simply a distasteful task that had to be done during a hard shift. I knew how to do that. I'd done it a million times. This time, however, I chose to keep my heart open in Hell.

I closed my eyes and sank into silence, and within that silence I chose to put up no barrier between myself and the raw stuff of Jimmy suffering, to let it wail forth and pass through me and not defend against it. And so it did—a rage and anguish in the violence of his cursing that could only be described as the anguish of God. I had never heard such a sound or, more accurately, had never allowed myself to hear it.

I suppose it's strange to speak of such a man as Christ, but to me it seems clear—not only the crucified God (myself playing the role of the Roman soldier) but also Christ the healer. Before my meeting with Jimmy, I confess there was a secret self that was confusing my work as a healer. If I didn't exactly believe I would save the world, I did think that I would somehow diminish its suffering by hard work and the extremity of my goodness. Jimmy healed me of that delusion. He delivered me to the day-by-day work of serving the sacred in whatever form it presents itself.

39
THE PEACEMAKER THAT HAS NO NAME

This is the way the spirits come to me. They trance possess me, come in visions and dreams, or come physically like this old man who had these herbs. So you see it is difficult to say how many spirits work through me. But the Peacemaker is the most powerful of the spirits. He is the one they obey. I call him the Peacemaker that has no name.

This particular spirit can trance possess anything. It can speak from a rock, from a tree or from human beings. The way it operates is strange, mysterious. At one point it trance possessed my little boy Moses. So you see it can speak through anybody. That is why it is unnameable. You cannot identify the source of this power. Michael was chosen by this spirit that he should follow the way of the Peacemaker. From this moment don't call Michael, Michael, and don't call Augustine, Augustine—they are to be called Peacemakers. That is what happens to a person who is ruled by this spirit. In truth the power who is the Peacemaker we've yet to understand. So we wait.

There's something special about what my spirits or, rather, the spirits of this world have taught me—to be submissive to them, that I should be their walking stick. They have taught me to love and respect all creatures; to respect and treat with compassion all the people of this world. They have even taught me to be under them, under all creatures, under all peoples of this world. Everything that lives must lead me. I am their child. They have taught me to pray so that there is peace for the world.

They have also taught me that the riches of this world are an obstacle because the more one gets in the form of the things that are of this world, the more problems one creates for oneself. We were born into this world, we found these riches here, and when we leave this world, we leave all the riches behind. The spirits have taught me to thank them for what I am.

40
A FOOL FOR SURE

When I was last in Africa, I had to express my gratitude to the Shona and Ndebele people who have truly taken me in as kin. I gathered together about thirty of us—all ages, old *ambuyas* and *sekirus*, little boys and girls. I told them, "Ever since I came, I keep hearing over and over Christ's words, 'Do not put your light under a bushel. Don't withhold from one another your gifts.' The gift you have given me is that you have made me a *nganga*. Augustine initiated me, but that did not make me a *nganga*. When you come to me with your suffering and your willingness to trust, my spirits come forth out of love, and they tell me how to heal. Without you I would know nothing of what it means to be a *nganga*, and in my life I've never wanted anything more than this."

After speaking, I washed everybody's face with rainwater. "Don't hide your light under a bushel," I said. "Take very good care of each other."

A mischievous spirit had me buy a few dozen fireworks, the kind that you dangle the fuse over the lip of a bottle and send flying in a spray of orange sparks. "God has a sense of humor," I explained.

One by one each of us lit a firework after saying a prayer that we wanted to send to the ancestors. One woman walked up with her sister, who could neither hear nor talk and offered a prayer on her behalf. For a second her face glowed, and she had sparks in her nappy hair. No bushel covering up that light!

When I thought we had finished, you called to me, "Michael! You have to send up a prayer also." I had completely forgotten myself.

I looked around at the expectant faces and reached for a prayer, but I only heard silence. Everybody's faces were so beautiful, and suddenly I understood that I was the tribe; all of us for one second the petals of a single flower.

Squatting down I lit the fuse. I raised my hands and chanted a prayer to celebrate the beauty of this flower—and the firework blew up in my face. I fell over and laughed until there were tears in my eyes.

In this life I am, for sure, a fool. There are worse fates. My childhood ambitions to become a saint have failed miserably. I have not become a saint, but I have learned a few things about kindness. I've learned that kindness is what one lives for. There's nothing else to live for. I've worked with dying people for over twenty years, and I know that when someone comes to the end of their life, the only thing that matters is how much they've learned to love and how willing they have been to be loved.

What I see often in America are people who will come to the end without having really learned a lot from being alive. To me this is the worst tragedy, far worse than death. The opportunity to learn to love was always there, and it was shut out. They die without ever knowing why they were alive in the first place. I see that quite often. I wish I could say it is uncommon. Sometimes I think it's normal in America.

The spirits have gifts, and we ourselves are gifts that the ancestors want to give to the world. The only thing to do with a gift is to pass it on. Happiness depends on being open to the gifts that are offered and to give them over with delight.

41
I AM HERE

You cannot separate ancestors from God. You can't. These are the faces of God. I agree with the Jewish scripture that says, "No graven images" because what people do is create an image and then worship that image, and it becomes a God. You cannot make a God. God is not an object. If you want to see the faces of God, look at a mountain. You will really see the power of the Creator. Look at another person; you will see God. But I don't pray to that person. I pray to the power that made that person and this mountain. Nobody is perfect. Nobody is righteous. We are all young babies. We stand up, and we fall. We stand up, and we fall.

I am not a perfect Augustine. I am not righteous. I am just being told to say things to God's people, to God's animals. This is my message. Over and over again, "I am here." It is all that I have to say.

AND THE STARS ARE HER CHILDREN
by Michael Ortiz Hill
for Joyce Dube

Egg split
the cleft spread wide
but what womb where
could carry
the children of Africa and Europe?
and who is this dark mother
we call Mambokadzi, Queen
who spawns twins such as you and I

Your wife's sister maddened with AIDS
Joyce wailing in the night
you don a leopard pelt
and douse her nappy head
while I sing her a song
to the Mother of Water

We carry her to the car
to drive the dry cow path
to her mother's mud hut

Greeting us at the gate
Amai sees not only her daughter's ravaged body
but hears in the bereft stuttering
her own mother's voice

"This child I cannot heal,"
says the spirit
as Amai wraps grandmother in ancient cloth
and bows respectfully before the old one

Daughters and mothers and grandmothers
and grandmothers of grandmothers
gathering singing and clapping

You told me once the Mambokadzi was the moon
and the stars are her children

to be born into poverty
to die young in poverty
to be anguished
and possessed of an anguished spirit

What does it mean to be a healer
in such a world, my brother?
The parched earth, the long lament
the Queen herself weeping
among the children of darkness and light?

How is it that her tears
become our tears
her dust our dust?

Grandmother and the dear woman
that housed her spirit
yields to the silence
of the slivered moon
and two ragged men
one black, one white
drive the blue Peugeot
into the darkest hour
of the night

AFTERWORD
DARE'—A HEALING COMMUNITY
by DEENA METZGER

When my husband, Michael Ortiz-Hill, first, and I, afterwards, went to Zimbabwe to be initiated by Augustine Kandemwa, we expected that our lives would be changed, but we did not expect to be educated in a way of healing that would be relevant for North Americans, actually providing a model to ease some of the most serious disruptions and dislocations of modern life.

Stopping over in Johannesburg on the way to Bulawayo, in December 1997, I had the following dream:

> The phone rang and I answered it. No one was there. It rang again. Again no one was there. The third time I heard a man's voice. He asked if I was Deena Metzger.
>
> As I answered, I was astonished that anyone would find me in this Johannesburg hotel as Michael and I had relied on a taxi driver to recommend lodgings. Even stranger, the deep voice belonged to an indigenous man from somewhere in South America.
>
> I asked, "Who could possibly know me in Johannesburg?" Ignoring my question, the man asked if I would carry the book made from the film, *The Heart of the World*, and if I would teach the pattern. "We have identified the pattern," the man said, "and we have used it and it has been effective."
>
> "What is the pattern?" I asked, trying to remember the details of the film that I had actually seen some years before and wondering if he was referring to something other than the establishment of harmonious relationships with the natural world. I wanted to ask specific questions, and I also wanted to describe the pattern as I imagined it, but I couldn't find the exact words.
>
> Then I said, "A friend of mine is with the Kogi Indians." I was mystified that I would receive this phone call while my friend of forty years, Victor Perera, a journalist, who has written about the Lacandon Maya, was possibly with the Kogi at that very moment. I had not spoken to my friend for some months, though after a long silence between us, he had called to tell me he would be visiting these people, to speak with

them, as he had with the Maya about the sacred wisdom tradition they carried.

I spoke with nervousness and confusion. The man re-
mained silent, disinterested in anything I said or asked. I
quieted myself.

He spoke. "There is little time. If this contact is right, I
will get the book to you tomorrow, Friday."

Still troubled by details, I began to review my plans for
the next day, then realized that all my plans were meaningless
in the face of this possibility. Then the man asked me what I
would pay for the book.

"Pay?" It seemed an absurd question. "What do you
want?" I asked, "a measly thirty dollars? If it is what you say it
is, I will give my entire life to it." I was deeply unnerved as I
hung up the phone.

Immediately I awakened as unnerved as I was in the dream, or more
so. I did not, could not, believe it was a dream. Though I had seen the
film, I did not know then that there was also a book written by Alan
Ereira, the BBC filmmaker.

It was our custom, when we were in Zimbabwe, to tell each other
our dreams each morning. The second day we were there, I told Augustine this dream about "the pattern" and *The Heart of the World*. After
meeting Augustine I realized that Spirit had brought all of us together to
create alliances that might contribute to the well-being and the healing of
the world. I did not feel that our meeting was either casual or personal. It
was remarkable to me that an American Jewish woman would be invited
to work alongside a black African healer. In the course of our work together, it also happened several times that we, Augustine, Michael, and
myself—joined by Patricia Langer, a remarkable healer from Toronto—
were in the company of other African healers, and we all worked with
and upon each other. We were learning to yield to each other's wisdom
and, in my husband's words, we were learning how "to serve each other's
spirits." This has been one of the great privileges and honors of my life.

Augustine heard the dream profoundly. He agreed that it was essential to create global networks of wise, initiated people who could, through
their alliance, protect the planet and alter the very destructive behavior
and consciousness of the ones the Kogi call "The Younger Brothers." He
speculated with us about the meaning of "the pattern." Augustine is a
humble man, but he has had many dreams and visions instructing him to

collaborate with other healers and to work with people across the globe. "The pattern," we all agreed, had something to do with creating a web of connection, a circle of relationship.

After participating in initiatory work with Augustine, Patricia and I traveled to South Africa where we had some other remarkable experiences which deepened my belief that the creation of a net of healers and healing, the creation of alliances between elders and wise ones among all peoples, particularly those who carry original wisdom, is the crucial work of this time. But also, I was instructed, not for the first time, that alliances with the natural world are possible and essential.

Just when I returned to the United States, hostilities broke out with Iraq. I was and continue to be alarmed by the global military threat. I began to propose councils of elders calling the wisest from all traditions to sit together, grieving, to yield to each other's wisdom, to see the way Spirit speaks differently but profoundly through all of us, to take responsibility together until we receive wisdom sufficient to alter the violent, destructive, and most greedy ways and consequences of "The Younger Brothers" who are ourselves. I thought then that these councils of elders were one form of "the pattern" I was instructed to teach. Here are some excerpts from the letters calling for such councils.

> The call for a global council or councils of elders as well as local councils of elders continues to be necessary. We must step out of all of our familiar and established ways of knowing and acting. The times are that urgent.
>
> I do not know if we will find ways to save ourselves, the animals, the trees, the earth from our own destructive patterns. I do not think that any government or known system or individual will accomplish it. I am asking you to stand with me at this terrible place of not knowing without pretending or hoping it is otherwise. Let us stand here. Open eyed. Grieving.
>
> There is no one thing I can point to that if it were healed, would be sufficient. All the systems mesh. We are caught in a destructive system with multiple manifestations: nuclear war; biological or chemical warfare; fascism; genocide of original peoples; religious, racial, and ethnic wars; terrorism; famines; urban despair; abject poverty; unprecedented incidents of mental illness, depression, psychosis among individuals—too many of them in positions of power—elected, inherited,

appointed, or seized; the decline of ethical concerns; the destruction of the rain forests; the pollution of the environment; the death of spirituality; the disappearance of plants and animals; meaninglessness—these are some of the signs of the system which acts against us.

In contrast there is a living net through which all beings sustain and nurture each other. We have somehow substituted the deadly net for the living one. As humans we have forgotten how to be part of such a living net. We have forgotten the way of it and also the beauty of it. Realistically, how can we return? What can be done?

We can search out each other's counsel. We can come together in unprecedented, inter-connecting global councils, seeking out the wisdom which is not in our own traditions or ways of knowing. We can stand together before the ruins of everything that matters without blaming each other but eager to find new ways. We can seek out those who are not like ourselves and find camaraderie and solace with them by confronting all of this. We can stand together open eyed and open hearted. Even if we are able to do nothing but put our own threatened and weary selves before the decline that is taking our children, the calves and pups and offspring of the animals, and all the seedlings, we will know that we set our own personal lives aside on behalf of all the creatures, for what matters most.

Small circles of peers sitting together in council, seeking each others' counsel, openly speaking grief and heartbreak, assisted when appropriate by prayer, contemplation and mediation, may be blessed with wisdom and understanding. Many of the elders on the planet know how to access the wisdom of Spirit and the natural world. Let us speak with each other.

The letters that I wrote distributed themselves across the world, and many people were inspired to gather together in small, intimate groups to seek council with each other in order to find ethical and humane ways to live their lives. Still, there were many days when I was anguished over the world situation. One day driving along the Pacific Ocean, I found myself weeping hopelessly. Then I heard a voice within me that was not my voice urging me not to despair. "It is not as difficult as you think," the voice said. "All you have to do is put the forms in place." "Who are you?" I asked. "We are the Sanhedrin," the voice answered. I understood that these were the spirits of my tradition, a council of the wise who had advised people for thousands of years, since the time of Moses.

I returned to Africa the next year with Michael and two of our colleagues, Michele Sang-O'Brien and Amanda Foulger. We went to Chobe in Botswana with Augustine, and I had an extraordinary encounter with an elephant. For years I had been dreaming of elephants and their predicament to the extent that I felt called to be with them. When I saw an elphant, I call "The Ambassador," move toward me from one half a mile away with clear determination—focused, deliberate, conscious, aware intention—I realized that everything I had ever thought about elephants and animals had to be reconsidered. This was even clearer when the elephant approached me and Michael on our knees in the open back of a pickup truck, bowed elaborately and then walked to within three feet of us to look directly in my eyes for over thirty minutes. A half hour later as we left the park, we were unmistakably acknowledged by a half-mile line of elephants that gathered just as we were driving out.

I had approached the elephants as another holocausted people and had been praying to sit with them in some kind of council so that we might make an alliance across species lines. In the presence of this elephant and in the company of Augustine and our colleagues, I felt as if I were being informed by remarkable beings about the ways and importance of kinship and family relationships.

This time when I returned from Africa, I felt compelled to establish *Dare'* in my community as an outgrowth of the Council of Elders. For several years I had been training healers both in Los Angeles and nationally in the creative, ethical, and spiritual aspects of healing. Now with the example of Augustine and his community, it was clearly time to enact the teachings. My Wednesday Morning Women's Healing Circle, which had been in existence for four years, took on the responsibility for *Dare'* with Michael and myself.

Directly informed by Augustine and his *Dare'*, we made the practice of invoking Spirit through drumming, voice, and dance central to our form. Additionally many of the principles of healing that we rely on are based on Augustine's teaching and example.

This is an excerpt from the original letter inviting the community to the first *Dare'* that would take place at Michael's and my small house in the Topanga hills in April, 1999.

Augustine Kandemwa, an indigenous Shona healer from
Zimbabwe, introduced Michael and Deena to the idea of *Dare*,
or Council. In Bulawayo, Zimbabwe's second largest city,
Augustine has re-imagined a tribal form in an urban setting.
Dare is a healing community. This means that *Dare* is a community where healing is the primary focus and concern and
exchange between the participants is constant and dynamic.
Increasingly we have come to the radical understanding that
all the members of the natural world rightly participate in
community with us. Augustine believes that many diseases
are caused by "the heaviness of the spirits upon us." The healer
acts on behalf of spirit, calling people forth, opening the path
between the individual and spirit, removing the obstacles to
the spiritual life. The ways of coming to spirit are many and
can be both arduous and beautiful. Song, prayer, and ritual
are as essential to the healing process as are medicine, treatment, dream interpretation, divination, and service.

In the Shona and Ndebele tradition, Spirit heals through
us. "I am God's feet, I am God's hands," Augustine likes to
say. The healer's task is to create himself or herself into the
vessel that can carry the healing spirit. In any given moment
the healing spirit passes through a room, and anyone who has
the capacity receives it on behalf of the community. The extraordinary healer is the one who is so devoted to the spirits
that he or she carries the spirits all the time for the sake of the
community. But ultimately, there is no great distinction between the healer and the one who needs healing. Just as the
beggar can be the angel who calls forth our gifts and generos-
ity, the one who is ill calls forth the healing spirits in the healer
as the healer invokes them in the one who is ill. Through
initiation one is both healed and empowered to bring healing
to the community. The members of the community learn to
heal each other; the one who receives is called forth to develop the capacity to return the gift. As the healer must be
sustained in order to heal, the question the community poses
to itself is: How can we sustain each other.

Healing is not a profession; it is a way of life. Exchange is
not limited by money or one's ability, and so the sacred and
beautiful are not commodified or commercialized. At this
terrible time, it is essential to re-imagine art, healing and
community. These gatherings are seeds for beginnings we

cannot yet conceptualize. The task is to see how we can each come forth to meet and ease each other's suffering and concerns.

We are deliberately trying to create a form without rules, protocols, minutes, legislation, organization, statements of purpose, grant applications, tax deductions, agendas. We are not charging anything for *Dare'* or any of the healing work that will take place within it. We assume that those who come will bring with them food and drink and whatever else might be necessary so that this day is completely successful.

But what we offer in whatever forms they manifest are: mediation, council, medicine, massage, energy work, conversation, shamanic work, curanderismo, divination, ritual ceremony, cooking, reading, gardening, prayer, poetry, dance, song, art, listening, silence...all leading to healing.

We will call each other forth, receive from each other in the ways we can and will offer to each other what we can. To receive what heals and to offer what sustains—this is the goal.

Dare' is based on the idea of the gift as a sacred responsibility. We are given gifts. These gifts are for the sake of the community. We add what we can to them. We pass them on. Such is the way of the authentic and meaningful life.

Dare' takes place from 1:00 p.m. to 9:00 p.m. on the first Sunday after the new moon each month.

There have been many times in the eighteen months since we established *Dare'* that I have felt exactly as I did in Africa. There, after a sweat, twenty-five or thirty of us gathered in Augustine's small *Dare'* room, one on top of the other, to listen to each other and to the spirits that were speaking through us. Adults, children packed together in a room telling dreams and singing, sometimes even dancing there, among the masks, skins, baskets, herbs and ritual objects which make the Zimbabwean *Dare'* a holy place.

Here in Topanga, where thirty or so gather around the round low table which has become a circle of animal spirits, it is the same but also different. We had to find a form that reflects the people who live in this area of the world. You can say that like Augustine, we listened to the spirits to find out how to proceed, to the many spirits that represent the many traditions in our area. It is our hope that we will become adept in all the healing languages so that we can honor, regain, restore, use, and preserve the traditions that we have lost. In this way, though, we are also in Augustine's tradition for he has welcomed each of us from different parts of the world so warmly and has asked us to teach him the wisdom of our lineages.

Earlier in the day, as in Africa, we meet outside because we find the presence of the land, creatures, and elements sustaining, and also because there is not enough room in the house for all the people who are usually with us in the afternoon. So far the weather spirits have been good to us.

The day begins with oracles. Usually Michael tells the cards, but sometimes I do as well. We are devoted to augury as a way of reading the intention of spirit or gaining guidance for the participants. We ask simple questions to orient those who come, some of whom are afflicted with serious physical or emotional illness or are suffering the ways so many people suffer in our culture from poverty, let's say, or loneliness or mean- inglessness. We ask: Where is this person at this moment? What path is spirit laying out before him/her? What is the first step? These questions invite stories, and the stories provide a foundation for the person to ex- amine his or her life.

We never know who will come to *Dare'*. There are always familiar faces, and there are always strangers. Once a stewardess that I met on an airplane came to *Dare'* and received the strength to challenge the medical industry that had refused tests and misdiagnosed her husband's ultimately fatal illness while coercing the sick man to prevent him from receiving alternative treatments. Another time we were blessed by a priestess from the Yoruba tradition devoted to Yemaya. We are fortunate that there are always people from traditions other than the dominant white culture who bring the richness of their heritage as well as the grief they carry. It is my task along with the women in the Healing Circle to greet those who come, to extend a warm and gentle welcome and to discover what need for healing or need to provide healing has brought them here. We shape the proceedings according to what the individual needs are and what is brought forth in the community sessions. We pay particular attention to the direction or inclinations of Spirit when we are together in order to see how to proceed and with whom.

Somewhere around 2:00 p.m. we begin to call Spirit. Someone brings out the big drum, Eve, that was given as a gift by the community to the community. Up to eight people at one time can keep the heartbeat on Eve. The other drums come out also along with the rattles and other

instruments. Introductions are made. Our intentions are spoken. Someone will begin. Perhaps I will call Spirit in my tradition, calling on the
Holy One in Hebrew to be with us. Or Amanda Foulger may step forward and call the four directions in the shamanic tradition. Once, Mike
Wimberly, an African American bass trombonist, played music he had
specially composed calling slaves forth to freedom. Or ChoQosh Auh-
Ho-Oh may blow on a conch shell as her Chumash people, indigenous
to California, did. Richard Grossman strikes a gong or blows a didgeridoo,
Netanya Selman awakens the crystal singing bowl, Sarah Vaughn picks
up the clarinet, and we begin. We don't know where the music will take
us. We turn to music, as Augustine instructed us, as an essential practice
of *Dare'* because it has been for millennia a form of prayer. We call the
Spirits and—we are grateful—they descend.

Afterwards we meet in small groups. Someone may lay on hands,
several practitioners offer massage, an acupuncturist may put up her table
in the grass under the eucalyptus trees while Stephan Hewitt, Carol
Sheppard, and Danilia Wild and others gather around the ill people and
sing into their bodies. Juliette Hanauer holds up her palms and energy
pours out of them and Ursula, Valerie Wolf's fourteen-year-old daughter, learns the way of laying on of hands. It is difficult to explain how
healing comes. Each time it is an original and wondrous event. But we
see the changes. A woman who is out of work finds a job. A woman who
has been very isolated in her community feels at home among us. A brain-
injured boy who did not develop past six months old celebrates his
fifteenth birthday with us, smiles and tries to drum on Eve. When, as so
often happens to him, he is in pain and distressed, Michael sings a Shona
prayer over him, does a little ritual work, and he seems to be eased. Another boy, ten years old, experiencing much difficulty in school, dances
like an angel and shows us his poems and drawings. The first time he
came, I asked him if he knew what prayer is. He said he did, and as I tied
African shell ankle bracelets around him, I asked him if his dance could
be a prayer. He said it could, and it was. Dina Fraboni, who teaches
sacred dance, moved alongside him, grateful that she has found a public
place where she can pray in her own way, and Margie Rosenblum assumed sacred yoga postures, which are her way of attuning to Spirit.

There is a man who was debilitated and depressed with AIDS who is
now living a quarter of a mile away, working as an actor and landscaper
and happier than he has ever been in his life. One man came to *Dare'* to

speak his grief over his wife who had just died, and two men joined him in council, both speaking of having given up several years of their lives to care for their dying parents. A man from Brazil stood up with a walking stick and limped around the circle like old man Legba while chanting in Portuguese for his recently murdered mother. A woman wailed the unmourned suicide of her brother one Passover eighteen years ago while another woman comforted her and secretly grieved the loss of her lover by chanting in Hebrew: "May this grief pass through you."

In the late afternoon, we sit in Council together. A talking stick is passed, and we address a question that is crucial to the community: experiences we have had with healing; how we live the conflict between our ethics and the impossible demands of our culture; how we survive in a workplace that is inhuman and unethical; times we feel we have been corrupted and undermined; what is our grief; what miracles we have witnessed; how do we heal each other?

We speak spontaneously and from the heart. Month after month as we share the deepest feelings and truths about ourselves, we change. Sometimes a person comes only to speak once and then never comes again, but sometimes we hear that their lives are different.

A man comes with an environmental disease; he is allergic to almost all chemicals. We speak to him as someone who is carrying a truth for us, a canary in a coal mine, showing us how we endanger ourselves with environmental devastation. He no longer feels like a pariah because he must stay outside, is made sick by carpets, furniture, cleansers, paints that are inside our houses. Someone offers him bodywork. Michael tells his cards. I counsel him. Valerie Wolf prays over him in the Native American tradition. A moving healing ritual occurs spontaneously, and at the end of it Michael kneels, singing in Shona and Ndebele and washes his feet. Weeks later we hear that he has found the energy to move to a house that is not infested with fungi. He is not entirely healed, but his life is better, and he is encouraged or at least not so discouraged. We pray for him.

We pray for the woman who has been told she has liver cancer. She is mounted by a Tibetan Buddhist spirit of fierce compassion. Month after month, she comes to *Dare*; she begins to sing after having silenced herself for over ten years. She begins to write. Her prose is passionate and lyrical. The novel she is working on proceeds. The doctor says her liver function tests can mean two things: she has liver cancer or she is undergoing a rapid and unprecedented healing. Suddenly she also requires surgery for cervical cancer. The community rallies around her at the hospital, attending her before, during, and after surgery. The doctor is asked if she can imagine that every cut and stitch is an act of healing, that she is not only a surgeon but also a healer, that she has the capacity to bring healing also through her presence. The doctor herself says she is honored to take this on. The surgery goes well. The woman recovers well. There is no liver cancer; her liver was healing. The woman says she could not have survived this without *Dare'*.

We meet in small groups again. Someone takes the children for a hike. Moriyah Colaine takes the young boy who dances for a stroll in the sage-covered hills. Others meditate. People gather around the food that everyone has brought. A man from Morocco puts a delicacy he has cooked into my mouth. The atmosphere is convivial. There are two men at the sink washing dishes together. A man and a woman are making a fruit salad. People consult each other to see how to live their lives. There are healers in the room from many different traditions who have not had the opportunity to practice their art. I tell people not to hold back on their loving. This is the place where we can offer back to the community and Spirit all the gifts that have been given to us.

Now it is time to meet together to end the evening. Night has fallen and fog is moving in over the hills like the ancestors returning. We gather in the small room feeling comfortable cramped against each other. Susie Green focuses healing energy onto a woman who is suffering from chronic fatigue syndrome. Someone massages someone else's feet. Asia speaks for the mountain lions that are endangered. Recognizing the animals as part of our community, someone takes a different endangered species each month and speaks on its behalf. The month I took the elephant, an elephant's trunk appeared in the clouds of the sky, and birds skittered brazenly through our circle as we drummed, toned, and danced.

People tell dreams. Gary Davidson dreams that a mountain lion jumped on his shoulders. We remember what Asia said about these animals. We think of Augustine who is lion totem—*Shumba*. We speak of this dream and others as indicating that the dreamer is undergoing shamanic initiation. Jim Deveraux speaks of what it has meant to have adopted as his son a young man, Solo, from Augustine's *Dare'*. Michael speaks of the violence that is tearing Zimbabwe apart before the elections. Someone begins chanting: "Africa. Africa." We all join in. The next week we hear that things are calmer. An anonymous donor has given a sum of money which is sufficient to buy a tractor for the African *Dare*. Eric Field says he is trying to raise tuition money for a young Masai man he met who wants to carry his people's healing tradition alongside medical training. Over the months that money is raised.

A woman who has been studying with me for some time joins us and decides to create *Dare* in Boulder, Colorado. It will be different there than it is here. She brings different gifts. She is a school psychologist, and she wants to incorporate the children into the *Dare*. She wants the little ones to take part in the Council. I think of the moment when my eight-year-old granddaughter, Jamie, told a dream she had to the group. "I dreamed I was an Indian and I didn't understand the white people in the funny clothes and hats when they came to our tents. When I woke up, I knew they were Pilgrims." She is perplexed but she laughs at herself, so identified with the Indians that she was unable to understand her own people, her own language in her dream. Another young woman, twenty years old, who has come for the first time, tells a dream of being arrested by Nazis. She was certain she would be shot and left to die in a mass grave. She has suffered with this and similar dreams for almost a year. We speak of what it means to carry the enormous suffering of the twentieth century and of our people, what it means to have the grief-stricken ancestors come to us in our dreams. We say that we will help her carry these dreams because they are too much for any individual, especially a young woman. Several men and women in the room are crying. I speak to the group of the traditions in which people dream for the community rather than for themselves. What it means to be a dreamer, like Simakuhle, Augustine's wife, who dreams the healing herbs for the well-being of the community. Jamie, with the gravity of an eight year old, turns to the young woman and gently touches her knee: "If I had a dream like that, I would get into my mommy's bed immediately and tell her my dream." "That is exactly what I did," the young woman responds.

It is time to say goodnight. We sit quietly while one after another speaks the names of different people in the community who are suffering or who have suffered losses. We hold the names. We pray for them. We pray for the trees and animals who are caught in the firestorms that are raging in the western states. We sit in silence. Perhaps someone sings a song and we all join in. Then it cannot be put off any longer. We must say goodnight. Some children are carried out asleep. There are hugs and handshakes. One more time we have spontaneously woven this group of strangers and kin into a community.

Patricia Langer has organized *Dare'* in Barrie, Canada, just outside of Toronto, and another *Dare'* in Saskatchewan. She and her students offer the ill in the community energy work and do healing sessions with them each week. When a child is born into the community, Patricia organizes a naming ceremony where the children call the fairies and bless Megan, the little one, who is named for the Fairy Queen. Patricia also gives teachings, and a community forms itself around these new/old ideas. Her students form healing teams that attend people who are in the hospital, and they do ritual and ceremonial work for those in need. Others who have attended *Dare'* from San Francisco speak of forming one there. "We will do it in the park," they say. Rachel Choppin wonders how to establish *Dare'* in Israel as Lela Koncar considers whether something like this, no matter how limited, might be established in her country, Croatia.

There is another aspect of *Dare'* for which we are grateful to Augustine. He taught us that *Dare'* is also a training ground where the process of healing is co-incident with becoming a healer. This is what it means when Augustine says that the spirits are heavy upon someone. It means that their illness or depression is a consequence of spirit calling them. Calling them to a rightful path, calling them to right relationship with the spirit world and calling them to be a healer. Without *Dare'* one could suffer confusion for a long time before understanding one's predicament. But in *Dare'* the teaching of the spirits are clear, and we learn quickly to read the signs and find our way.

Each of the *Dare's* is different because they are shaped in response to the culture and people who are in them. But they are also based on common principles. Perhaps we can say that what we all do wherever *Dare'* exists is "putting the forms in place" and "teaching the patterns."

When we told Augustine that *Dare's* were being established in North America and that some of the participants were even dreaming about him, he was amazed. "I didn't know my spirits traveled so far," he said, laughing that exuberant laugh of his which is healing in its own right.